Turkey

Turkey

A Sketch of Turkish History by Freya Stark

Photographs by Fulvio Roiter

with 168 plates   25 in colour

Thames and Hudson   London

The notes on the plates are based
on material supplied by Fulvio Roiter

Gravure illustrations printed in Switzerland by Imago, Zurich
Text printed in Switzerland by Druckerei Winterthur AG, Winterthur
Bound in Holland by Van Rijmenam N. V., The Hague

ISBN 0 500 24074 4

To my dear hosts
Sevim and Memduh Moran

Contents

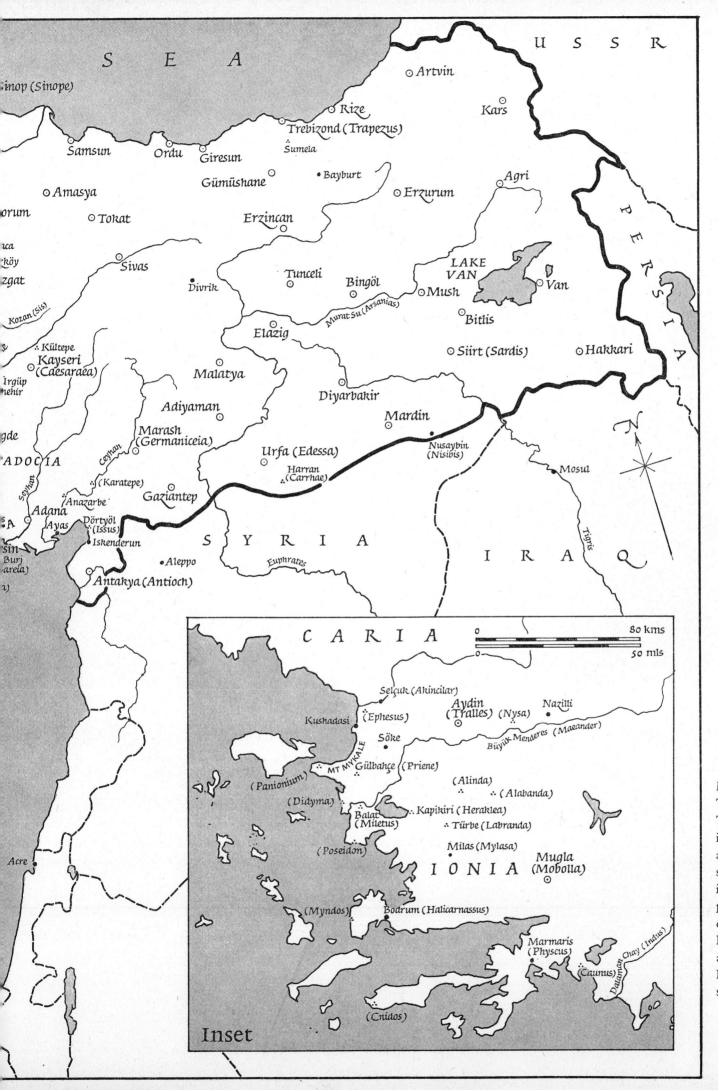

SEA

Sinop (Sinope)

Samsun   Ordu   Giresun
○ Amasya
orum
○ Tokat   Gümüshane   • Bayburt
ca
köy
zgat   Sivas   Erzincan
Kozan (Sis)   • Divrik   Tunceli   Bingöl
:. Kültepe   ○   ○ Mush
Kayseri   Elazig   Murat Su (Arsanias)
(Caesaraea)
Irgüp   Malatya
nehir   Diyarbakir
gde
                        Adiyaman   Mardin
ADOCIA   Marash
                (Germaniceia)   Urfa (Edessa)   Nusaybin
        :. (Karatepe)   Harran   (Nisibis)
    ; Anazarbe   Gaziantep   :. (Carrhae)
Adana Dörtyöl
sin Ayas (Issus)
Burj • Iskenderun   S Y R I A   I R A Q
areia)   • Aleppo   Euphrates
  Antakya (Antioch)

• Artvin

Rize   Kars
Trebizond (Trapezus)
:. Sumela

            Agri
    ○ Erzurum

                    LAKE
                    VAN
                            ○ Van

                        • Bitlis

    ○ Siirt (Sardis)   ○ Hakkari

                                    • Mosul

                                        N

                                    Tigris

U S S R

P E R S I A

Acre •

CARIA   0   80 kms

                                            50 mls

            Selçuk (Akincilar)
                        Aydin   • Nazilli
Kushadasi :. (Ephesus) (Tralles) (Nysa)
                Söke   Büyük Menderes (Maeander)
MT MYKALE
Gülbahçe (Priene)
(Panionium)   (Alinda)
                                :. (Alabanda)
(Didyma)
Balat • Kapikiri (Heraklea)
(Miletus) :. Türbe (Labranda)
(Poseidon) Milas (Mylasa)
                        Mugla
I O N I A   (Mobolla)
                            ○
(Myndos) Bodrum (Halicarnassus)

                Marmaris
                (Physcus)
                        :. (Caunus)
                                    Dalaman Chay (Indus)

(Cnidos)

Inset

Map of
Turkey.
Three dots
indicate
ancient
sites; a dot
in a circle,
provincial
capitals.
For the boxed
area round
Istanbul,
see page 12.

1 Istanbul: Everyday Life on the Bosphorus

A palimpsest, my dictionary tells me, is 'a manuscript which has been twice written on, the first writing having been partly erased'. This definition is not, I believe, absolutely correct, because there might be several writings underneath, and it would still be a palimpsest; and whatever the library variety may be for the learned, the traveller's is always of this more complicated sort.

Every country is a volume of such kind, its incomplete quality is a chief ingredient in the excitement and interest of travel. Its secrets delve into freedoms equal to the open freedoms of the surface world, though with a difference, and one might never want to travel at all if one could reach in one's own back yard the level of events in Balkh or Babylonia or any other place that has buried some record behind it.

The palimpsest does not, however, delve into the secrets: it presents a past that has worn through to visibility, whose ancient lettering presses through the dominant script of the modern world, and – though no more than a flourish here and there – emerges clear enough to weave its varied texture in Time, of movement and pursuit, escape and capture.

> *What leaf-fring'd legend haunts about thy shape*
> *Of deities or mortals, or of both,*
> *In Tempe or the dales of Arcady?*
> *What men or gods are these? What maidens loth?*
> *What mad pursuit? What struggle to escape?*
> *What pipes and timbrels? What wild ecstasy?*

John Keats put into this whole ode his evocation of the palimpsest, the breaking through of past into present – our hoarded riches.

During the last fifteen years or so, I have usually spent a part of my summers in Turkey. A little watercolour in my study, by some last-century amateur, not very competent but full of humility and feeling, looks out from the shore of Asia towards Seraglio Point. The landscape has now mostly altered and become crowded with new things: the wall that stretches along the coast-line, from the oldest strip built by Constantine below St Sophia, through the few carefully collected remnants of the Imperial Palace, to the sea-tower at the south-western end, has now

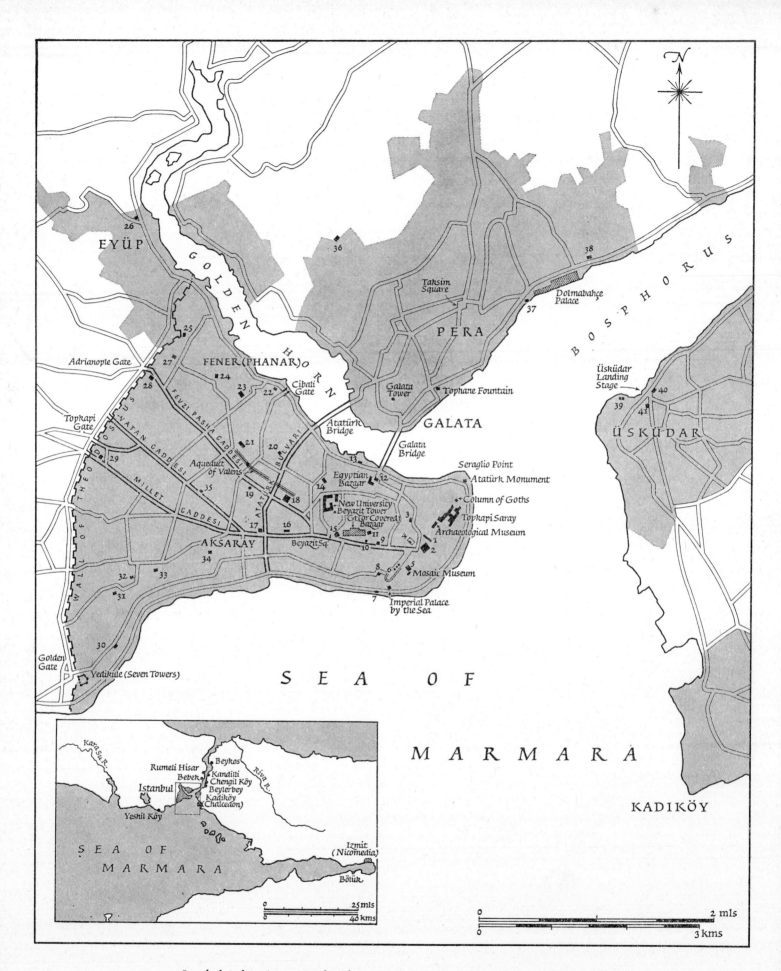

Istanbul and environs. Numbered monuments are listed opposite. Cami = Mosque.

cleared away its little hovels of rubbish, and strides with a boulevard beside it; and beyond it, the houses have extended year by year towards Yeshil Köy,* the 'Green Village' of the aerodrome. The detail has changed, but the outline remains, and nothing can spoil the domes and minarets of the horizon: St Sophia, Sultan Ahmet, Beyazit by the university tower, and Suleymaniye beside its tombs, the queen of Istanbul; and bending with the curve of the Golden Horn, Fatih the Conqueror's mosque, and Selim the Grim; Mihrimah, the last of this glorious rank, built by a princess and one of the most simply beautiful, is out of sight. As one sails into the Bosphorus from the Islands of Princes after bathing, the domes look in the sunset like the richness of earth, and the minarets are winged to heaven. Now there is a point along the Bosphorus road on the Asiatic side where an ancient Jewish cemetery has by some miracle kept an open space of grassy hillside, and the view has not changed since my sketch was painted; and often, when I have driven down to Beylerbey at the waterside, in a bus or a car or a 'dolmush' (which is that excellent compromise whereby you pay only for that one of the five seats which you happen to occupy, and which London Transport is, I am told, thinking of copying), I have sent a thought to the tourist-artist sitting there with his paints and brushes on one of the forgotten tombstones a hundred years ago.

Unlike the western, the eastern side of the Bosphorus is not so very changed. The villages, still dimly lighted, let one clatter under their plane trees through cobbled streets – Chengil Köy, Vaniköy, Kandilli, Anadolu Hisar. At this last, beyond Sultan Beyazit's Asiatic fortress and with the towers of Rumeli Hisar across the water, I find a welcome among friends in an old house at the water's edge. The bell rings from the tarmac road above, where owls at night sometimes sit on the long connecting wire and waken the inhabitants; and easy steps lead down to a little patio, to the front door and the highway of the water. Sun and salt and the wet winters have bleached the pinewood walls almost to whiteness, but they are solid enough, and so are the inner beams of Anatolian oak. From this hospitable door, the family pours out with easy, faithful welcome, the servants come smiling to kiss the guest's hand and touch it with their foreheads; life is flowing from its antiquated pattern into the modern changes, and novelties and traditions together weave the charm.

The house is all ups and downs, with a wide curving staircase and saloon above, and vaulted kitchen where such comforts as frigidaires stand like islands. It is a summer residence, and things few and simple as possible are brought and carried back to town at the end of the season. But bits of taste and splendour survive from the early nineteenth century, when most of these Bosphorus houses were built: a meander of black and white cobbles makes the pattern to an entrance, and water piped along the upright hillside tinkles along a carving of branches to splash a pleasant noise from cup to cup into its marble basin.

My own room has five high windows arched to the ceiling. Their curtains, tattered by the Pontic winds, spread sheets of sunlight across the clean scrubbed floor. Apart from the absolutely

---

*For the spelling of Turkish names, the following procedure has been adopted: the ç and ş of modern Turkish have been rendered, respectively, as ch (pronounced as in church) and sh (pronounced as in ship); the modified ö and ü (pronounced as in German) have been retained; and the dotless ı (representing a sound somewhere between ö and ü) has been treated as an ordinary i.

necessary furniture for sleeping, and two opposing sofas, there is nothing to interfere with the noble proportions of this room. The walls are bare, and the ceiling alone is decorated with thin geometric wands of painted wood laid on stucco in those pale colours of beige and green which the Ottoman century loved; and the light and air and Black Sea summer breezes linger in this shelter on their way. Under the window, the Bosphorus hurtles small waves that rise like tossing hands where the current changes – where gulls and cormorants dip and show the run of the *palamut* downstream.

These, and the sword-fish (*kilich*), are the Black Sea's best, and better than all the Mediterranean can offer. Fishermen draw in their boat to our steps as we breakfast on the patio, and cut them into slices; the blood flows red like meat, because of its freshness, and looks naturally Byzantine on these shores where so much blood has been shed.

The days are peace now, shut away between low banks that rise to Balkan and Anatolian uplands and solitudes out of sight. The city can be seen in glimpses at a distance, and washes past us in black and white steamers whose home is round Galata Bridge; the men of our house prefer to cross in a boat to Bebek and return in the long summer light from their offices in time for a bathe. I myself am terrified of the current, which here is apt to turn suddenly and without warning and, with those tossing hands which might be those of all the odalisques floating up for vengeance, would carry one straight down to Seraglio Point. In 1595, when Mehmet III inherited the throne, nineteen brothers and nine pregnant concubines were eliminated at one go. Young people swim across, and so did my godsons, but I followed in a boat, anxious to increase our visibility and reluctant to see those beloved heads, so small in the waves, scalloped off by some tanker on its way. A Russian one, when I was there, took the Bosphorus bank in a fog, annihilating a house and the people asleep inside it; the long outlines, built low for oil, majestic and silent, drift down like the Lady of Shallott with never a sign of Russian life on deck.

We women of the house live on our patio in bathing dress or wrapper, with the garden climbing behind us to the unseen road, and books or letters are led astray by the constant fascination of the water. Sometime in the leisure of the morning, Gül announces a bath, and leads with soap and towels to where wooden clogs stand on the threshold of the bathroom's shadowy corners and stone floor. Triangles of daylight are let rather dimly into the ceiling dome; and as one stands naked there, Gül with a brass dish pours the warm water over neck and shoulders while it overlaps its marble bowl round our feet. She soaps one's back into the phantom ease of childhood, passive in nanny's hand. Gül, whose name is Turkish for rose, was not like nanny; she was a tough young peasant wife from the far eastern edge of Erzincan, with a little girl of three, the household pet, who would creep round our table like a mouse when her bedtime came, to touch the hand of master or guest with her forehead for goodnight. She had the eyes of her father who waited on us, dark pools of wonder; but Gül was as clear, fair and positive as the wild rose of her name, and talked in some strident eastern dialect I found it almost impossible to follow. 'Shall we soap a third time?' she would ask, having scrubbed with the rough glove twice already: she was doubtful of western cleanliness.

The variety of the day called at our watersteps: boats with vegetable sellers crying their wares, or burners of charcoal, or those who spend their time piling the highland logs for fuel, or the manicurist or the masseur on their weekly round from one mooring place to another.

Visitors dropped in at all hours, except those of the siesta; or we ourselves, constricted in clothing, called at one or another of the waterside houses, or walked up the valley to the Sweet Waters of Asia, a sluggish stream now sadly modernized, or visited the Polish refugees in their century-old village on its height.

The Bosphorus is no help for the visiting of Istanbul itself. In two years or so, they say, a bridge will be built across it, and the Asiatic shore will become as noisy and as strident as the western; but at present, if one goes by car, one must wait for a ferry either at Üsküdar or Beykos, and that is frequently a matter of hours. If one has no car it is easy enough to step across the gangway onto one of the little steamers, and sit under an awning over a turquoise-spotted glass of tea: but after that come dust and jostling decanted among the trams of the Golden Horn, and the streets have sudden habits – if you are looking for the less-visited monuments – of turning from asphalt to small boulders underfoot. Few of the sustainments in an oriental city allow one to sit down: the sellers of ground-nuts or chestnuts, according to the season, do their trade standing; the provider of fish at lunch time, in his unsteady boat at the quayside, fries on a primus and reaches out delicious slices wrapped in pink toilet paper to the office boys on the embankment; only the water-pipe or narghile is good for all seasons and offers the support of two extra chairs for one's arms, and brass tongs on a tray to manipulate the tobacco and cool it as it travels upwards. The narghile, however, is restricted to men (in public), and its habitués are found in quiet places, nearly always under trees, such as the café behind the mosque of Beyazit, where a street of books runs into the Great Bazaar.

The Great Bazaar, in spite of a good deal of jostling, is still refreshing in shadow and comparatively cool with water sprinkled on the ground. It is restful, though, only if one can leave the main thoroughfares of jewellers glittering with bangles, the wide windows of sellers of quilts and bolsters embroidered on western satins, where the patterns known to the Mongols survive here and there (the palimpsest comes through), the long arcades of hideous furniture, carpet backgrounds stacked in twilight, black and white goatwool rugs of Zakho, the corner-stands of slippers glittering with tinsel, and the gaiety – when the month for circumcision draws near – of sashes and white skull-caps embroidered in silver, which the tiny boy will wear when this first great ceremony of his life comes round.

A strange mixture of pain and pride must remain in the child's memory of the splendour with which every family tries in varying degrees to celebrate his status. It gives confidence perhaps to have this matter so incisively accentuated and must strengthen an awareness – scarcely needing much encouragement in Turkey – of the general superiority of men. We of the subjugated sex are happy to resign to our amiable menfolk a mastery which, in their Istanbul offices in July, entails all the heat and labour of the day. Far from the glittering windows, by alleys so high and narrow that our skirts brush both sides as we walk, we find a row of workshops built in walls that once enclosed ecclesiastical prisons in the Byzantine state. Here the chiselling of the best jewels is still carried on: perched on boxes, we watch while our friend the jeweller – his brother and apprentices crowding to share the enjoyment – pulls out from what looks like a casual drawer the treasures of his hand. If not the oldest profession in the world, the jewellers must obviously have followed closely. Their delicate filigrees trip down the ages, earliest witness to the slavery of women, since every ornament we wear – ring, bracelet, chain – is named after a shackle: yet how agreeable, all the same! From our bags we produce the knick-knacks that need a pearl or two, or perhaps have to be melted down and altered altogether, and while that is being considered we can handle the so femininely tough, brittle and lasting sprays that hang their diamonds like petrified dewdrops on trembling artificial stems. They need more embroidery, chiffons, and leisure than our age can give them to look their best.

There are other secluded corners I like to visit in the bazaar: a tiny room up a very steep stair, where Hellenistic pottery from Pergamon or Myrina found its way to a happy man who loved his polished terracotta wares and would have given them to me at unreasonable prices if his brother had not been by to stiffen him. And there was George, in a little tree-shaded court out of the bustle, who knew all about coins and let one spend an hour looking at them for fun, and – alas! – in all the troubles has disappeared.

There is no durable escape from troubles in the eastern Mediterranean (or anywhere else for that matter), and the old Russian who owned a treasury of carpets had to be tracked to a room protected by blank walls in a tortuous labyrinth off the Istiklal Caddesi (once the Rue de Péra). All these visits were more than mere buying and selling: one enjoys them for something that is not simple acquisition, but a part of whatever the art that one is pursuing may be. Thus X, who is a bandit and despoils people like an octopus in the darkness of his cave, once said: 'You must not think that we do not care for the beauties of life', and drove me to the view from Chamlija, where the Bosphorus and its history lie spread out in the sun before one.

I spent a month of sightseeing in Istanbul when first I went there. The kindest of friends offered the Embassy Rolls-Royce to go about in; but it soon became obvious that the streets I liked were too narrow, and we were in fact too grand, and I took to walking, tiring myself like any sentinel along the walls, picking up bits of antiquity that are now almost obliterated in the Greek Phanar quarter of the city, along the Golden Horn, fascinated by all footsteps that leave a trace behind them and are meant to be followed, or any stair with a door left open, where the mystery of the background gives dignity to the figure that emerges, as if it were desert or the sea.

Now that I have wandered into most parts of the old city, I am inclined in hot weather to revisit places where one can sit down. The Yerebatan was one of these: one could hire a boat and float in coolness among the underground colonnades of Justinian's water supply; but this has been stopped (people probably got lost, since the Istanbul underground reservoirs must cover an area almost equal to that of the ancient city). All one can do now is to stand on a wooden platform and see the conquered temple columns and the Byzantine brickwork lose themselves in long vistas of shallow water-shadows. Even so it is one of the most evocative things in Istanbul.

The temples were destroyed not only by Christians but by earthquakes, and then the Byzantines too were conquered, and what is left of their little churches is being carefully restored. But since they are not much prayed in, there are no seats – no quiet people as in Italian churches, sitting alone for their moments of meditation and repose. And the mosaics that remain are mostly, apart from the greatest, clustered in small corrugated domes over one's head, enchanting but not easy to look at; so that it is more restful to both body and spirit to make for a mosque.

How cleverly, apart from religion, these have been thought out for repose! One's shoes are off and one sits anywhere, and the carpeted floor gives no echo of walking feet to distract, and the windows open only to a colonnaded court and its fountain, or shed their shafts across the empty spaces of the dome. Throughout the intervals of the five daily prayers, one can sleep in a gentle atmosphere of help, or meditation, or, in a corner where the light falls, sit swaying gently with lips moving to the words of the Quran.

Suleymaniye, built by Sinan, the greatest of the architects, for Suleyman, the greatest of the Ottoman caliphs, is the climax of the city of the Muslims as Justinian's St Sophia was for that of the Byzantines. Not comparable inside with the absolute proportions of St Sophia, which is queen of all, it is far more beautiful outside; and an obscure little tea-house overlapping onto the opposite pavement allows one to sit there for hours, following the great domes and the ridges descending from turret to turret, and the little domes and windows in their order, as if it were Kachenjunga or Everest before one, a part of the architecture and purpose of the world.

The mosque spreads itself too, into kitchens, libraries and lodgings for students, and an arcaded school which is now one of the pleasantest of small museums, all carpets and calligraphy, lecterns for Qurans, book-bindings, or pen-cases, a glow of gold-leaf and colour to cast round the aridities of learning. The other buildings have lost their earlier uses, but keep themselves sober in grey stone on quiet streets, so that the atmosphere if not the substance of their intentions is still there, and it comes to one's mind how passionately devoted these caliphs were to education in all its branches, how Selim the Grim wrote poetry as well as executing almost every one of his prime ministers and deposing his father, and how Suleyman, though he killed his two sons, is one of the few rulers who freed the learned from the payment of taxes altogether.

Hundreds of other mosques are ready for the visitor to step into, and one of the best is that of Suleyman's vizier, Sokullu Mehmet Pasha, who survived him and carried on the tradition of the great reign for a little while through the depravities of its successors. He, like the Hellenistic kings before him, thought of joining Red Sea and Mediterranean when the Suez Canal had already been obvious to history for nearly two thousand years. His mosque is all light, with a cloistered approach of cupolas some way below the rather ordinary beauties of the Blue Mosque above; the light falls into it through coloured glass set in stucco in the eastern way, onto the brightest patterns of sixteenth-century tiles.

Not far is the 'Small St Sophia', the Justinian sixth-century church of SS. Sergius and Bacchus, with a Byzantine air which no subsequent Muslim alterations can destroy. There are hundreds of other mosques – both in Scutari (Üsküdar) across the waters and in the city walls – great or small, like the Shehzade, named after Suleyman's murdered son, or Rustem Pasha, loveliest for tiled ceramic walls, or Mustafa Pasha where the pigeons can drink on a small pillar of their own while the faithful wash hands and feet below.

The mosque I came to know best was the Yeni Cami (also called the Yeni Valide), because it was near the place where steamers of the Bosphorus take off below Galata Bridge. The letter-writers sit beside it with typewriters on portable tables, collecting the world's sorrows from peasant women writing to their soldiers on a frontier, or from old countrymen who follow the unexpected styles of their simple requests with anxious furrowed face. Beyond them are the charming ways of the small, roofed-in bazaar known as the Egyptian Bazaar, where the Venetians once sold spices, and between them and a chaos of trams and cars the wide mosque platform makes a walk for pigeons of the same grey colour as the stone. With time before my boat left, I would step into the twilight of the tiled walls that stand like a blue night in their shadows, and sit there while a few women strolled in when the evening lengthened and, seeing me alone, came quietly and friendly to talk of this and that. The dust of the day was over; my boat left with the last city workers, with tea for those who wanted it, and circular rolls scattered with aniseed they call *simit*, and many odd objects – combs, safety pins, shammy leathers, feather dusters – for sale up and down the decks to keep the passengers amused.

It was a short walk in the dark from Anadolu, the prettiest of all the villages, clustered round its castle and already settling for the night. The Bosphorus lay still as lakewater below the road, the lights from Bebek in tremulous columns across it. When I looked out before reaching my bed across the length of my room, the air had begun to waken and freshen in the night; and when I was safely asleep, if a steamer passed silent down the current, a load of waves would hit my foundations, and the scrunch of water would be like sacks of gravel thrown against the shore. The current scrabbled and swalled and shifted under my bed and the thin planks beneath it, as if a shaggy tame animal were settling in its lair, and as the unseen ship went on, one could hear or imagine its smooth wake hitting the shore in ever diminishing distance till it faded under the city in the south.

1 View from the Suleymaniye mosque, Istanbul, looking across the Bosphorus to the shore of Asia. On the left can be seen part of Galata Bridge, and near the centre the Yeni Cami (New Mosque), also known as the Yeni Valide Sultana (New Queen Mother) mosque.

2–3 The quay just below Galata Bridge is a headquarters for steamers that carry commuter traffic up and down the Bosphorus and to and from the neighbouring Marmara Islands, while on the other side they travel up the waters of the Golden Horn. This very efficiently organized service is here seen in operation against the background of Galata Bridge and the Yeni Cami, with the Nuruosmaniye mosque beyond it.

4 The summer season stretches from May to October. It draws tourists and inhabitants from Istanbul to the European shore of the Bosphorus, and especially along those twelve miles from Bebek to the Black Sea where a cool and pleasant breeze is always blowing. On this, the more sophisticated shore, there are excellent hotels and plenty of restaurants, whose speciality is fish.

5, 6, 7 The gate and towers of Rumeli Hisar (six miles from Istanbul) are still intact, and look out to the Bosphorus where it is narrowest (550 feet), half way between the Black Sea and the Sea of Marmara. The castle was built by Mehmet the Conqueror on land rented from the shrunken realm of the Byzantine emperor before the actual siege of Constantinople began (1453), and when the castle of Anadolu Hisar, built by Sultan Beyazit, already held the Asiatic shore.

This noble fortress – built in less than four months, it is said – is still used as a summer theatre, where Shakespeare plays are often given, and where the Janissaries in their old uniforms reappear with their drums and standards on Sunday afternoons.

8, 9 The old-fashioned Bosphorus traffic, moving up and down its banks or criss-crossing between Europe and Asia – the traffic of the caiques with their bright colours, primitive lading, and waists low in the water – is already threatened by the bridge whose first stone was laid in February 1970. By 1973, a bridge of almost a mile in length is promised, uniting Europe and Asia.

10, 11 The *yalis*, or wooden houses along the Bosphorus, were built in the eighteenth or nineteenth century with beams of Anatolian oak and walls of pine which the storms that pour down from the winter steppes have bleached to silver. The citizens of Istanbul bring out their furniture and live in them in summer; but since the building of a wooden *yali* is now forbidden, because they very easily catch fire, the cement and mortar of new bungalows is gradually replacing their delicate and expensive workmanship.

12, 14 The entrance to the Sokullu Mehmet Pasha mosque, erected on the supposed site of the church of St Anastasia, which had been founded by Constantine the Great. The mosque was built in 1571 by the architect Sinan, by order of the daughter of Sultan Selim II; and it is dedicated to the memory of the great vizier who served and survived Suleyman the Magnificent, and carried on his renown and his conquests under the miserable authority of his half Russian son. Most of the Sokullu buildings and traditions are in and around Edirne, where his campaigns against the Bulgars were fought, but the Sokullu in Istanbul has a peculiar charm of lightness, quiet and economic beauty. The sandals have been left by worshippers entering the mosque.

13 The Sultan Ahmet or Blue Mosque, built by Mehmet Aga between 1609 and 1616 astride the ancient Hippodrome and the Byzantine Imperial Palace,

is now the principal though not the most beautiful mosque in Istanbul. It has the peculiarity of having six minarets, and was, until well into the last century, the point of departure for the Mecca caravans. Its great chandelier, no longer fed with oil but electrified, is lit every night at the time of the evening prayer.

15   Cupolas of the courtyard of the Suleymaniye. The most sumptuous and beautiful of all the mosques of Istanbul, it was built by Sinan, the greatest of the Ottoman architects, between 1550 and 1556. The great prayer-space is a rectangle under a painted cupola, newly restored and resting on four pilasters – with two semi-cupolas to take part of the weight, as in St Sophia. Close by is the tomb of the too-much-loved wife Roxelana, whose intrigues killed the Sultan's young heir and brought her own son to the throne.

16, 18–19   The mosque of Eyüp has all the characteristics of a place of pilgrimage. At the end of the courtyard a green door opens to the tomb, one of the most venerated in all Turkey. The disciple of the Prophet, Eyüp, was killed during one of the early Arab sieges (AD 670) under the walls of Constantinople, and his tomb was lost during the centuries and forgotten: until, the legend has it, his voice cried out for victory during the fight along the walls when the Janissaries broke through. The body was rediscovered in 1453, and the Conqueror visited it and built a mosque and tomb.

Ever since this event, a new sultan would visit the tomb a few days after his accession to be girt with the sword of Othman.

17, 20   The ceremony of circumcision is the chief rite in the early life of the Muslim boy, and is celebrated with as much hospitality and pomp as his family can afford. A white skull-cap, embroidered with silver and many other ornaments, is worn for this occasion, and every guest is expected to bring a gift.

21   The delight of the narghile – hubble-bubble, *qalian* – is known by all Turks, old and young. The tobacco is placed, together with some red-hot embers of charcoal, in the upper part of the contrivance, and the smoke, before reaching the devotee, filters and loses its asperities through the water in the container on the floor.

22, 23   The Covered Market, or Great Bazaar, is a city within the city. It has its fountains and small mosque, and a kiosk where one can climb a narrow stair and drink tea and look through windows at the milling crowd below. Although prices have risen very steeply, one can still enjoy oneself and pick up oddments in the Bedestan, or flea market.

24   The Sea of Marmara, seen from the Seven Towers (Yedikule) – where unpopular ambassadors were once liable to be imprisoned.

9

The highlands of Anatolia on their western edge slope gently to peninsulas and valleys, hillsides where the figs of Smyrna and Halicarnassus can ripen, with innumerable inlets for the coming and going of ships. But the southern coast is abrupt, and the wall of Taurus, an unbroken skyline as far as the eye alone is concerned (for the passes are hidden), runs like a bastion above the Phoenician sea. Its two plains, Pamphylia and Cilicia, are niches that open from the far steep sides, and lie round deltas of rivers burrowing to low and sandy beaches, and this is all fertile land from the bay of Antioch westward, except for the huge hump of the Rough Cilicia, from Silifke to Ghazi Pasha, hostile and little inhabited through the ages.

This is rich soil now, growing vegetables in Pamphylia, for Ankara and other lesser towns, or dedicated to cotton on the Cilician plain. The swamps have mostly disappeared, though some of them still lie thick with mosquitoes round castles that once held the Syrian marches: Anazarbe and Sis and Toprak and Yilan Kalesi (Fortress of Snakes) on their hills. Ayas, at one time the most popular of the medieval harbours, has also vanished, shifted between the moving sands of rivers whose banks are never still. This was a tricky coast a century and a half ago, when Captain Beaufort, commander of HMS *Frederiksteen*, surveyed it for the Admiralty, and in his civilized Regency manner, copying Greek inscriptions as he found them, discussed with his officers the locations of classical names. There is an asphalt highroad now, but it pleases me to think that I still travelled with Beaufort's map for reference, with all its coastal detail so carefully and beautifully drawn and all the inland completely blank – his useful work having been interrupted by a wound collected during an attack by bandits in the Ayas marshes.

When I travelled along this coast in 1954, the Rough Cilicia was hospitable and friendly as everything else in Turkey, although foreigners even then were practically unknown and a crowd would gather at the door of any *lokanta* where I happened to eat. But the Smooth Cilicia, spread between the highland gates and Adana and Tarsus, was already sophisticated with banks and developing harbours; and round Mersin there never seemed to be a landscape without a foreground of women stooping, in lines of anything up to a dozen or so, hoeing young crops of maize or cotton under the eyes of some village headman (presumably), who stood watching them with the fat of the land around him, against the purple background of the hills.

Professor John Garstang, a gay and learned archaeologist and my friend, dug into the mound of Yümük Tepe close to Mersin, and published a book about it, *Prehistoric Mersin (Oxford)*, in 1953. It is still, I believe, one of the standard records for the Early Neolithic and indispensable to the study of this type of civilization south of the Taurus: but it means more than that to people like me, whom the minute varieties of potsherds – momentous as they certainly are – leave, imaginatively speaking, cold. There are pages and pages of the contours of pots in this beguiling book, but they can be skipped, and Garstang asks the reader's indulgence in that he regards archaeology, 'not as an end in itself, but as an index to human endeavour, with its failures and its general progress' (p. 9). This he succeeds in expressing, uncovering the history of the little mound from Arab-Byzantine (AD 300–1500), through the eastern Greek (1200–500 BC) and Hittite (1450–1200 BC), to the Chalcolithic copper age of the third millennium, and finally to where the Early Neolithic vanishes into Time on the ground level of the river and the plain. It lived here on what was to become a route for trades and armies, from Mesopotamia or Syria by the Calycadnus (Gök Su) valley to the plateau – the easiest of the passes – which Cyrus and his Ten Thousand and the Crusaders followed in later times.

Bernard Berenson once remarked to me that he thought the happiness of mankind to decline with every removal from the Neolithic. This little society of the mound had twenty or more centuries in which to develop in peaceful isolation with no necessity to fortify its homes. One sees its members building the earliest dry-walled houses, discovering the cultivation of cereals, learning to domesticate animals, to weave and paint their pottery, and spin. They begin to shape the corner-stones of their sheepfolds, to press small pebbles to harden the mud of their floors; to build walls solid enough to stand over three feet, which was all that the first inhabitants could manage. As Garstang notes, 'The even firing of pottery remained a problem long after other processes had been mastered' (as it still was in South Arabia thirty years ago), and the idea of a jug had not yet come to them, though they could burnish vessels to make them less porous; the small marks of women's fingers are left where the rim turns. A heap of Neolithic debris was accumulated through the centuries to nearly ten metres' depth, with not many changes: a lack of originality and outside stimulus, Garstang suggests.

Yet the slow changes came: the foundations of their houses became more symmetrical; stones used in the upper courses were packed with pebbles for solidity; painted pottery began before the end of the Neolithic age. Obsidian blades and axes of green stone beautifully smooth were their tools. The first grindstone appears for the crushing of grain, which became vitally important in the Chalcolithic age: and spindle-whorls, lumps of clay with holes to pierce them, still used today, show that weaving had been discovered; on the level where the Neolithic ends are the first rounded foundations of silos for the storing of corn.

Another lapse of at least a thousand years led through the Chalcolithic age, from 4000 BC or before, with still no break of continuity in the quiet process of its seasons, but with a gradual development of detail: the corner-stones of walls, the invention of baked bricks, foreign evidences in decorative patterns, possibly the result of visits from traders passing towards the north. A threshing floor appears, of beaten earth such as I have slept on when riding through remote villages of the upper Euphrates near Adiyaman, where the earth turns to brick of its own accord in the sun. Here the Palaeolithic left its tools, where later Persian-Greeks of Commagene built tombs and statues, and Rome her roads and bridges through the early and forgotten tracks of man. Stone implements and the obsidian began to dwindle, and metal gradually appeared. A distinctive kind of pottery known as Halafian revolutionized the local craft, and demonstrated or foreshadowed the end of isolation; and by the middle of the Chalcolithic era the first fortifications and a heap of human bodies showed that one stimulus at any rate, whose absence Garstang had noticed, that of violence, was now there. The period of peaceful progress was at an end; a citadel, carefully planned for defence by unknown but extremely competent invaders, came into operation, in whose domestic life, continuing on the old lines, women evidently survived.

As late as 1956, when Professor Seton Lloyd wrote his excellent little Pelican *Early Anatolia*, it was thought that the Neolithic had not crossed to the north of the Taurus. But it was found at Hajilar, and especially at Çatal Hüyük, thirty-two miles south-east of Konya, by Mr James Mellaart, who in 1961 began the excavation of this the most ancient city yet found in Turkey and one of the oldest in the world. His work still remains uncompleted; and since its interest concerns the whole history of mankind, one hopes that he may soon go on from where he left off – in the seventh millennium – to reach the level of the plain.

It was then already a city, inhabited by an apparently mixed race of as yet uncertain origin – hunters and agriculturalists enriched through the black obsidian which we have seen trickling down to Mersin, and whose layers stretch from the volcanoes of Konya to those of Van or Erzurum. The sparkling sharp pebbles push through roadside banks as far as Kars and probably into Russia, but the Konya supply came from the western end of the line, where Hasan Dagh, a two-peaked volcano, is visible from the mound of Çatal Hüyük itself.

Two thousand years before Mersin had learnt to build a wall, this commercial metropolis covered about thirty-two acres with closely packed buildings. The basic ingredients for civilization surrounded it: upland watered valleys where the originals of later cereals could be found, wild game to domesticate or hunt on the salty Konya plain, and the raw materials from which axes, arrows, knives and sickles for the cutting of harvests were made; there is evidence for the export of obsidian as early as 8300 BC.

The obsidian trade (with Jericho) continued right through the eighth millennium until, by the middle of the seventh, the momentous transition from stone to ceramics had started, and much of this central human procedure, from stone to clay, lies hidden in the unexplored earth of Çatal Hüyük. What has been excavated shows a prosperous Stone Age commercial centre, with metal beginning, with wooden utensils varied and sophisticated, and woollen textiles developed (the sheep appears to have been the first domesticated wild animal). The houses were sun-dried mud, set into wooden moulds – as they still are in South Arabia. The flat roofs were reed under mud, as in Mesopotamia; light could penetrate through little windows under the eaves. The staircase was a ladder and an opening in the roof (which also served as chimney and is still to be found in the north). Domestic life was probably very much what any traveller in the East finds today in out of the way places, with the universal eastern comfort of the divan provided by platforms for reclining, and matting placed beneath the cushions. Later Turkish-Tudor walls of brick in wooden frameworks are already foreshadowed, probably derived from walls entirely timber in a forested land: they could already rise to an interior height of ten feet a couple of thousand years before the early three-foot walls of Mersin had begun to grow.

Every third room would be a shrine, decorated with paint that often imitated weaving: a place with no trace of sacrifice, but some evident holiness in plaster reliefs and sculptured female breasts or bulls' heads endlessly repeated, and figures of riders, or of women giving birth – sacred symbols that develop through the seventh millennium, from some long Palaeolithic past of whose art hitherto nothing in Turkey is known beyond a few rock-engravings in the neighbourhood of Antalya.

It is a ritual art developed by hunting people, who had discovered agriculture and left the nomad life, and were making an earliest experiment in cities. The wonder of this revolution was still with them, and their domestication of the bull was recent enough to carry magic. According to Mellaart, 'Sometime during the fifty-eighth century BC, agriculture finally triumphed over the age-old occupation of hunting, and with it the power of women increased: this much is clear from the almost total disappearance of male statues in the cult, a process which, beginning in Çatal Hüyük, reaches its climax in the somewhat later cultures of Hajilar' (*Çatal Hüyük*, London 1967, p. 176). The usefulness of women appears to have been discovered, and the Mother Goddess has reigned ever since, with usefulness the basis of her worship – a thing which it is perhaps as well to remember.

Even apart from their theology, however, the people of this seventh millennium were artists already, pursuing their own creative pleasure: there is a quality Michelangelo might have recognized in the sculptured figures, and the painting of the dancers on the east wall of the Hunting Shrine (shrine A.III.I) might have been found three thousand years later in Crete. Most interesting perhaps of all is the single landscape – the first, I believe, known in the world and certainly the first discovered on a man-built wall – from shrine VII.14. Painted soon after 6200 BC, it shows the town, and behind it the erupting volcano – Hasan Dagh with two summits, 10,600 feet high – with little dots covering its side, and curved lines of fire issuing from its top. It is as abstruse as a modern picture to recognize, but there it is, clear enough to the generation that painted it: for the volcano remained active for another five thousand years, giver of obsidian, dangerous and uncontrolled and no doubt worshipped as a god.

After 5600 BC, the mound of Çatal Hüyük was abandoned, for what reason is not known, except that it seems to have been a peaceful one. There is no evidence of any massacre, and the site where the inhabitants settled is nearly as large as the mound they had left, and lies across the river, still unexplored.

The Bronze Age

The destruction of the golden age near Mersin, and the building of the fortress on its mound, happened during the fourth millennium, two thousand years and more after the blossoming of art on the plateau that I have just described. During all this time, people in Anatolia no doubt increased and travelled, and at the end of another thousand years, on the threshold of the Bronze Age, had developed the typical oriental contrast of squalor and splendour which makes it difficult to judge of any of their societies until some privileged tomb (as at Alaca) has been found. Travel they did, however, leaving their pottery as the frail thread of their journeys, though no place-name is satisfactorily authenticated until the beginning of the second millennium BC. Where they came from and when is still uncertain except for obvious links of contact with Syria and Mesopotamia for the south. The lands north of Taurus were probably visited either from Caucasus or Caspian, or across the straits from south-west Russia or Europe, while the Aegean coasts from earliest times looked towards the sea. From generation to generation the imperceptible development continued, blossoming with peaceful but unprogressive sameness in indigenous federations about which very little is known. In many cases, even their location is obscure. The Hittite tablets speak of them: Assuwa, along the Marmara coast; Kizzuwadna, including Adana and Tarsus; Arzawa, the most powerful Hittite opponent in the west. They were there, to be incorporated or dismembered by the Hittites when they came.

In the 1930s, and during World War II, when Turkey was neutral, excellent Turkish archaeologists entered the lists, and a number of the Early Bronze Age sites were investigated, from the western coasts to the Black Sea and eastern borders round Erzurum and Van. The most important finds were the royal tombs at Alaca, whose furniture – now in Ankara museum – caused almost as great a sensation as that of the Queen's tomb of Ur in Iraq. After the war, Professor Seton Lloyd uncovered a thousand years – about six building-levels from Early Bronze to the Homeric Age – at Beije Sultan, near the sources of the Maeander river. In a high pastoral country of shallow valleys in whose grassy bays the treeless villages shelter from the sweep of the Anatolian winds, he found a palace 'almost as large as the palaces of Minoan Crete' (*Early Anatolia*). It must have stood in the obscure territories of Arzawa, and flourished in the Middle Bronze Age with riches which have vanished, burnt and looted, so that little ornament remains beyond fragments of wooden pillars, plastered and painted, and less of comfort, beyond the traces of central heating (very necessary up there). The destruction seems to have happened about 1750 BC, and the place fell into poverty until the thirteenth century, when a new but less splendid palace arose, contemporary with the Hittite empire, and with the Homeric sort of stabling that suits the age of the Trojan War.

Prehistory was over, and, with writing, the Hittite tablets and inscriptions throw their light. But the story they tell is that of the Hittites themselves, and not of the nations that surrounded them, whose defeated silence would still be almost unbroken but for one of the cataclysms that seem usual after the discovery of metals – the burning, evidently sudden, of a suburb close to the mound of Kültepe in Cappadocia, where a colony of Assyrian merchants had been trading through the nineteenth century BC.

The East leaves much to be desired in ways of transport, but has always been expert in the management of caravans; and though horses were not used and camels had not yet been discovered, troops of donkeys – indigenous in northern Iraq – came up from Asshur by way of Sinjar, across the Khabur swamps and westward along the desert fringe to Harran (later Carrhae) and the modern crossing of the Euphrates at Birejik, through Gaziantep and Marash and the swelling hills of Cappadocia, to the high plateau where cross-roads for trading have probably existed from the first. The merchants of Kültepe were there to receive and dispatch this traffic, which went on for generations with no record of hazard, robbery or failure. They intermarried with the Anatolians, and lived in houses which were now founded on stone under sun-dried brick and wooden beams, and sometimes two-storied, as many are today. When their disaster came upon them they fled in haste, and left over a thousand clay tablets of purely business correspondence behind them, from which such details as we have, of Hittite predecessors and neighbours, are chiefly derived.

The Hittites, during the great movement of Indo-European migration, had made a slow progress to the west, and must have taken some centuries to reach Anatolia; Indo-European names trickling through the Assyrian tablets show how gradual and unnoticed a development it was. When they were finally sufficiently established to leave tablets of their own, they wrote down a record of fourteen kings, from the eighteenth to the fifteenth centuries BC, as founders of the Old Kingdom. Their language by this time had become mixed with languages and dialects with which it was surrounded, and the very name of their centre – Hattusas, city of the Hatti – was taken from an indigenous federation they had subdued, and indeed had cursed. Before the sixteenth century BC, they had moved most of their government out from the first capital at Kussara (perhaps present-day Alaca Hüyük), and seen the foundations of their empire established.

Lightning conquests of Aleppo and (temporarily) of Babylon, wars against eastern neighbours and constant forays in north and west are too numerous for this sketch, and it is better to close with a glimpse of Hattusas – Boghazköy or Boghazkale, as one may like to call it – where an atmosphere of great and virile power hovers over four imperial temples whose foundations alone remain. Over four miles of wall, by which the enlarged city was surrounded, remain with glacis, tunnelled passage and lion gates, embraced by precipitous gorges. The citadel is rebuilt on the site of the third millennium Hattusas; the village climbs below it, and long straight valleys easy for the descent and return of raiders point to north and south. These valleys, when I drove there late in summer, were filled with ripe corn that shone in the low sun like a wet sword. With the Hittites, the quiet Neolithic gods seemed dead indeed.

Even more than in the lion gateways and tremendous walls of Hattusas, the military feeling of the Hittites inhabits a place across the gorge which the Turks call Yazilikaya, the Written Rocks, at whose entrance the Hittite soldiers carved in rank make one think of the goose-step, and in whose natural refuge, on grey stone above the flowers, a sculptured empty panoply of the Dagger God appears, a robot whose backbone is a sword. The weather gods are near by, and the 'Young God' holds the Hittite king in an embrace not unlike a throttling.

The remarkable thing about these sculptures is that, when the inscriptions came to be translated, the names of the gods turned out to be not Hittite but Hurrian, a neighbouring language possibly brought by a wife who was known to have come from what is now Kurdistan in the east.

The Mitanni, breeders of horses, lived 'between the rivers', Tigris and Euphrates. North of these, roaming to Van across the unimpeded steppe and its volcanoes, the Urartians, or Chaldians (*not* Chaldaeans), known as the best workers of iron, left their stone pier and rock-cut tombs and cuneiform inscriptions against the rock that rises from the lake. They bring us down to the end of the second millennium and beyond it. The Iron Age is covering the Bronze and giving a brutal power to Assyria; and the Anatolian world has changed. The defeated Hittites have spread south to northern Syria and over the slopes of Taurus, ever more interspersed with local princelings, and united by a common resistance to the enemy at their gates. In 876 BC they were conquered, but were almost continually revolting, until towards the end of the century Sargon II subjugated them one by one. Yet their fading power left statues and rock carvings in greater numbers than ever, and the long-sought-for translation (Phoenician) of the Hittite language belongs to this declining time, engraved by an eighth-century king on the lions of his gateway, and discovered by a Turkish expedition at Karatepe in Cilicia in 1953. It declares his Greek, rather uncertain descent from the prophet Mopsus, whose legend one can follow at intervals down from the north.

The people he ruled were called Danuna, another possible connection with the Greeks (Danaoi) at Troy. When the Hittite power declined and the Phrygian had stepped into its empty spaces in the north, the coasts of what is now Turkey were already familiar with the black ships of the merchants and raiders from the west.

25   Çatal Hüyük: fragment from the dancers painting on the east wall of shrine A. III.1, the Hunting
Shrine, showing a hunter in white loin-cloth and black-
spotted leopard skin; round his neck he wears a pend-
ant, and in his right hand he holds a bow. Three digging
seasons, 1961–63, have opened out at Çatal Hüyük
what may prove to be the earliest Neolithic *city* in the
history of mankind. Thirty-two miles south-east of
Konya, towards the southern drop of the plateau, it lies
below a 65-foot mound and was discovered by Professor James Mellaart, whose scientific dating fixes it to
the seventh millennium BC.

It was by no means a primitive settlement, and re-
presents an immense progress from Palaeolithic times,
remains of which also exist in Anatolia. The commercial community that inhabited it had prospered on the
working and the export of obsidian, whose bright cutting edge, suitable for tools, can be found scattered
round volcanoes from Mount Argaeus (Erciyas) to the
neighbourhood of Ararat and Van.

Çatal Hüyük was a real urban environment, with
mud-brick houses arranged in a regular plan. There
were also temples, workshops and store-rooms. Most
of the objects brought to light – frescoes, sculpture,
utensils finely carved in wood, and jewellery – are now
in the Ankara museum. Only a third of the site has been
excavated, so that even more ancient discoveries may
be hoped for.

26, 27, 28   The village of Boghazköy (also known as
Boghazkale) lies below the hill where ancient walls still
encircle the capital of the Hittites, Hattusas. The strategic
value of the site is clear even to the non-military eye,
for the wide valleys open both north and south, visible
in all their detail to the city's sentinels. The place is
about 125 miles from Ankara, to the north-west,
branching south from the Samsun road.

The discovery of the Hittite civilization is very recent,
and any accurate information had to wait on the long
search for a clue to the language. Stray finds of Hittite
remains in the early nineteenth century attracted little
notice, but by the 1880s they were being systematically
recorded and examined, and in 1900 the first corpus of
Hittite inscriptions was published. Excavations at Hattusas began in 1906; ten thousand cuneiform tablets
were discovered. Work on the language is still in progress, but a point has been reached when most of the
historical texts can be understood, though religious
inscriptions still present problems.

The origin of this people remains obscure, beyond
the fact that they were newcomers either from north-
west or east; but the mass of information recorded in
their city, when once it could be deciphered, shows a
warrior nation with strong capacities for administration and imperial rule. Having destroyed the power of
the Hatti, their predecessors at Alaca Hüyük some
twenty-five miles away, they spread over the whole
centre of Anatolia and southward into Syria. In the
thirteenth century BC, their power began to break up
as the Phrygian peoples developed in the north-west.

The citadel at Hattusas, with the storm-god's temple
looking across to it and the city at its feet, still gives
the casual traveller an impression of vast solidity and
power: 'In the whole panorama of centuries, ... the
central historical fact is the existence for several centuries in the late second millennium of a great imperial
power, centred on the plateau, but extending its influence over much of the peninsula' (Seton Lloyd, *Early
Anatolia*, p. 4).

29   At about one mile from Boghazköy village, a road
leads to the rock-cut Hittite sanctuary of Yazilikaya.
Carved by nature into almost vertical walls, in an extraordinary atmosphere of strength and remoteness, relief

figures of the gods increase in scale as one goes further into the sanctuary, until one reaches the chief god Teshub, standing armed, and the goddess Hepatu wearing a cylindrical tiara and riding a lion.

30, 31 Yazilikaya. The entrance to the defile is guarded by marching armies, strangely modern to those of us who have lived through the wars in Europe.

32 Yazilikaya. In an inner sanctuary is the relief of King Tudhaliya IV (c. 1250 BC), in the embrace of a god much larger than himself (the 'Young God').

33 A late Hittite relief, with strong Assyrian influence, at Ivriz, off the Konya-Adana main road. King Warbalawa of Tuwanuva – a small kingdom near the modern village of Bor on the Nigde–Kayseri road – is thanking his god for the good things of life he distributes. The god, wearing a horned headdress, holds corn in his left hand and a bunch of grapes in his right. The Hittites by this time (about 745–727 BC, in the reign of the Assyrian Tiglath Pileser III) were breaking up and drifting south in many small principalities.

34 The Euphrates. This great river, 1,700 miles in length, begins as a broken-up stream in the Taurus (it is seen here near Adiyaman). Then it flows across the deserty plains of Mesopotamia, drawing its waters from a vast area and eventually joining the Tigris 100 miles from the shores of the Persian Gulf. This last tract is the Shatt-el-Arab, and the important international oil installations are on its eastern (Persian) shore.

The waters of the Euphrates rise at the end of March and subside through the summer to reach their lowest point in November. It is a curious fact that there is now not a single important city along its banks, while the Tigris still waters Mosul and Baghdad.

35 Adiyaman-Eski Kahta. This splendid bridge, which now rather seems to be leading from nowhere to nowhere, was built in 196 BC under the emperor Septimius Severus over the River Kahta (ancient Nymphaios), during the general tightening of the Roman Euphrates frontier against the Parthians.

36–37, 38, 39 Nimrud Dagh. On a mountain in south-eastern Turkey, over 7,000 feet above sea level, stands the 50-foot-high tumulus of Antiochus, the first of the Seleucid princess of Commagene. This line of kings, descended from Alexander's general Seleucus, ruled over a prosperous little kingdom, which owed its importance to the fact that it controlled two Euphrates crossings. It was swallowed in AD 18 by Rome under Tiberius, though Antiochus IV temporarily recovered it under Caligula, who was his friend.

The tumulus is four hours' journey (and it means mostly walking) from the hamlet of Eski Kahta. Around it sit the gods of Antiochus I, with their stone eagles and their altars and carved lions (pl. 39) before them, and a view that embraces almost the whole of his domain.

In 1881 Karl Sester, a German engineer, discovered this sanctuary, but being in a hurry could spend no more than an hour there. In 1883 two other travellers succeeded in reaching the summit and left an accurate description of it. The tumulus has now been excavated, and is well known but not much visited. The calm beauty of the sculpture – interesting because of its mixture of Persian and Hellenistic traditions – and the lonely grandeur of the site make its visit one of the most unforgettable experiences in the whole of Turkey.

The photographs show the platform below the tumulus, where the heads of the statues have now all rolled. The last to go was the garlanded Fortune of Commagene (on the right in pl. 38), which was thrown down by lightning in 1963. Originally they stood between 26 and 32 feet high.

40–41 Harran, close to the site of the battle of Carrhae (53 BC), celebrated long before that as a centre for the worship of the moon-goddess, and the place where Abraham sojourned on his journey from Mesopotamia to Palestine, is just north of what is now the Syrian border. Its beehive huts, built in a country deprived of timber, grow more familiar as one travels further west, but Harran is slowly dying for want of water. The remains of a castle, city-walls, mosque and school, excavated by Professor Storm Rice, show that in the Arab Middle Ages it was a flourishing city.

42 The long ridge of the fortress of Van dominates the lake and the rich, flat meadows that lie along its eastern shore. The castle itself is built of mud and must often have been rebuilt into quite recent times. But the rock-carved tombs and cyclopean harbour-wall go back into an antiquity known chiefly through the Urartians – a powerful people who from the eleventh century BC made this their capital, and fought Assyria on the south and the Kimmerians on the north.

43 Cuneiform inscription made under Xerxes on the vertical rock walls of Van in the fifth century BC. The text is given in three languages, Persian, Mede and Babylonian. By this date the Urartians had been overcome by the powerful empire of the Achaemenid Persians.

44 The Euphrates has two sources, the Kara and the Murat Su, the latter – the ancient Arsanias – rising east of the Tigris, and the former south-east of the Araxes. The Kara Su comes down from the north into the

Erzurum plain and flows into the Murat Su a little above Malatya, whence a series of the most stupendous gorges enclose it almost to its source.

A small jagged range between the Tigris and the Euphrates has been the unknown bulwark of Mesopotamia since its first creation: for the flooding of the two rivers comes at an interval of a month from one to the other, and has allowed the biblical land to form itself out of the river silt; if by any chance the snows were to melt a month earlier in the far uplands of the Euphrates, or a month later around the Gölcük lake where the Tigris is born, the two floods coming simultaneously would create a second deluge in the flat lands below. This photograph shows the Euphrates as it flows through the mountainous region of Erzincan.

45, 46–47   It is not difficult, though it is slow, to travel over great distances from one Turkish village to the next. Usually there is a bus or lorry, and surprisingly often a hard-metalled road, necessary if the winter climate of the north-east is to be dealt with. And if all these fail, the garry, with its tough little horses, fills the gap. The long, swelling lines of the north-east are here seen linking one volcano with another across great slopes of lava.

48   The ruins of Gordium: a city whose wealth and importance was ensured by its strategic position on the Royal Road, the great artery of trade between Asia and the Aegean. Its site was identified as Yassihüyük by the German archaeologists Gustav and Adolf Koerte. It was the Phrygian capital and the site of Alexander the Great's cutting of the legendary knot. Its identification has not yet been confirmed by inscriptions from the site, but there is no doubt of its correctness.

The Phrygians were a people speaking an Indo-European language, who began to immigrate into Asia Minor about 1200 BC, at the time of the Trojan War and towards the end of the Hittite empire. They occupied western Anatolia and became a political power under King Midas (738–696 BC). Having expanded the Phrygian kingdom to central Anatolia and become known to the Assyrians and Urartians in the east and to the Greeks in the west, Midas's power was ruined by the invasions of the Kimmerians, groups of nomadic horsemen who raided Anatolia in the seventh century BC. Midas remained a legendary figure to the Greeks, who spoke of his fabulous wealth and told stories about his golden touch and ass's ears.

The site of Gordium was first excavated by the brothers Koerte in a summer campaign in 1900. Excavations were resumed on a large scale by the University of Pennsylvania Museum in 1950, under the direction of Professor Rodney S. Young.

31

'When they were now entered within the deep haven, they furled their sails and laid them within the black ship, and lowered the mast by the forestays and brought it to the crutch with speed, and rowed her with oars to the anchorage. Then they cast out the mooring stones and made fast the hawsers, and so themselves went forth onto the sea-beach, and forth they brought the hecatomb for the far-darter Apollo … from the sea-faring ship…. And when the sun went down and darkness came on them, they laid them to sleep beside the ship's hawsers; and when rosy-fingered Dawn appeared, the child of morning, then set they sail for the wide camp of the Achaians; and Apollo, the Far-darter, sent them a favouring gale. They set up their mast and spread the white sails forth, and the wind filled the sail's belly and the dark wave sang loud about the stem as the ship made way, and she sped across the wave, accomplishing her journey.' (*Iliad*, I, 424–30, 458–67, translated Lang, Leaf and Myers, London 1949.)

Homer must have grown up with this scene – visible no doubt in the times he sang of as well as in his own – on any of the small Ionian beaches. One can still watch it in Levantine inlets, with little change except for the chug of an auxiliary engine now added to the silent gliding of the sail. In most places, during the intervening spell, a quayside has been built, and the fishing boats can find a metal ring or perhaps some old shaft of marble column to tie up to; and the ships have now acquired a peaceful middle-aged roundness, not combative but useful, while the 'swallows', the slim pirate craft that used to dart from Cilician hiding places, have disappeared.

If the eye is accustomed, and the imagination is awake, one can still recognize, even from a distance, anchorages or beaches that once tempted the roving seamen. They would be of two sorts along the coasts of Asia Minor: low headlands for the traders who could drag their ships across some isthmus with not too steep a gradient, and so get the protection of a north shore or a southern, according to the direction of the winds; or inlets which some high citadel protected, where the native sentinel could see far-off vessels approaching, and give notice, for attack or defence as the case might be, to his fleet of corsairs in some creek below.

These two different types roughly differentiate the anchorage of businessman or robber; and most of the commercial cities which developed along the northerly coasts of Anatolia clustered round the low headlands I have described. Here the Mycenaean traders, and later colonizers,

Aeolians, Ionians, Dorians, laid the foundations of Hellenistic Asia and Byzantine Rome. But in the south, whose intercourse from prehistoric times had ever been chiefly with Palestine and Syria and the open deserty spaces that led to Mesopotamia, and where the geography also helped with high, jutting headlands of Taurus, the pirate state was the more usual, and the cities that became prosperous in the level places were almost certain to base a good part of their incomes on the pirates' patronage and trade.

Such is Soli (Pompeiopolis when Pompey had settled it later with the repentant corsairs) – where Alexander stayed to review his forces and hold his games – now scarce a village, with only twenty-three columns of its colonnaded streets still standing when I threaded my path among brambles and sat by the silted shallowness of its petrified harbour some fifteen years ago. Because its inhabitants spoke Greek so badly, it has given the word 'solecism' to our language, and it lived prosperously between the trade routes of the south and the pirate slopes on its doorstep. A new road beside it now carries easily to Seleuceia (Silifke), and a BP summer camp completes the work of the late Roman world which in its day flooded out the traces of earlier settlers with a ribbon development of aqueducts, tombs, and the mediocre walls that followed the peaceful Antonines.

Out of sight, on the slopes above and with a view of nothing but sea and scrub struggling through cracks of the limestone, there is a whole region of tombs and stone-paved streets of the heavily carved, richly florid Greco-Roman age, where the priestly city of Diocaesareia suns itself, with theatre and triumphal gate and temple – columns standing, and an echo of quiet municipal prosperity about it which these cities carried from the heroic through the municipal into their decline. Such little towns, gently decaying, were already described by Marcus Aurelius writing to his tutor in the days of the Antonines, and there are scores of them in Turkey, still hidden among their almost impossible thorns. Our book, however, is intended for easy travel, and if it leads through the Rough Cilicia at all, must do so along the asphalt, which now swings high up above the pirate inlets, round sun-drenched solitary ridges of cistus and lavender, or pine.

The road reaches the southernmost tip of the country, where the bay of Anamur opens a magic curve of remoteness and beauty; we hurry on regretfully, with a short pause only for Roman Anemurium under the western crags – a city chiefly of barrel-vaulted tombs whose endless repetition makes one suddenly realize the boredom of the Roman peace before the barbarians came. Selinti (Ghazi Pasha) is west of Anemurium, with a river which had no bridge. I was carried across to see all that remains: 110 column bases of Trajan's mausoleum. There the old emperor died, and his wife and a few friends kept the death secret to give Hadrian time to post from his frontier and seize the imperial heritage, and I remember thinking how alive the place must then have been in the morning shadow of the fortified cliff beside its tidal bay of shining sand.

Alanya is still, but only just, in the pirate country, along an easy road lined with indiscriminate remnants of the last classic age. The great natural fortress, ancient Coracesium, lifts out of the flatness, crowned with Islamic walls, Byzantine and Seljuk, with only one gateway more ancient – useful and unobtrusive as the classic Greek fortification seems ever to have been. The legends if not the buildings have come down the ages, and Alanya is said to have been the last fortress to surrender to Pompey when the pirates were subdued. The character of the place remained – shaped by the nature of the sea-facing cliffs – in monuments Byzantine or left by later Karamanli sultans, when the Muslim raiders were as adventurous as their predecessors. Their narrow sea-swallows, 'with three masts and a bowsprit and triangular sails', were still seen in use by Colonel Leake, who travelled in 1800, and better lodged than ever in the galley slips left by the Karamanlis, beautiful and intact on the edge of the bay.

The Rough Cilicia ends and Pamphylia begins, and we reach the Hellenic world again at Side. Arrian, Alexander's biographer, says that its people were colonists from the coast of Cyme farther north, but adds that they 'talked a foreign language straightaway' (I. 26. 4) and became foreigners, so that it looks as if there had been a mixture in the first place, or at any rate as if business with their neighbours was intimate and brisk. It certainly became so, and the pirates' prisoners would be auctioned in the markets of Side, or sent, later, to the island of Delos, which became the greatest depot for slaves in the Roman age. Alliances with the pirates were scarcely a matter of choice with the Rough Cilicia so near, where 120 castles were eventually taken and 700 ships collected undamaged for Pompey's triumph. The friendship, whether voluntary or not, was profitable while it lasted; and when the lawless spell was over, the city still grew rich on agriculture and commerce, with two harbours now silted and shallow, and water from its long stone aqueduct cut through the gorges that frame its northern sky. Its houses bask in the sun, pleasantly scattered among ruins, with friendly people, most of them recent immigrants from Crete. Of all the cities of this coast it is the one most liked and inhabited by foreigners, where the ancient and the modern world have embraced in a gentle harmony that belongs to both and neither.

From the upper steps of the great theatre, the eye follows the beaches of Pamphylia and the whole width of the well-watered province to its hill-border, and when I first went there a wrestling match was to be held on a clearing, among fallen pediments and columns of the theatre floor. The young athletes were not unworthy of the long and famous sport that has been brought them by the wars and conquests of their past – a little more solidly built perhaps than those of Olympia, but with good straight looks and simple minds – and both the umpire (with his oil and water cans handy) and the marble faces carved among the ruins, faces of audiences long vanished, seemed to me to look with the same anxious appraisal at the subtleties of the game. In the August sun, the portico that surrounds the theatre threw its welcome gigantic shadows; and only the comparative silence of the crowd inside, ranged on their ancient seats, made one realize that a new picture had set itself into the old Mediterranean frame.

The feeling of Side is Greek now, whatever the people's language and sympathies may once have been; and when I first went there, the beautiful statues found among the ruins stood on a little open terrace looking wistfully across the alien Phoenician sea. Aspendos (modern Balkiz), the next city to the west, is Roman, and its theatre is rather like a magnified box, although the best-preserved Roman theatre in the world. On its inner façade, among small pediments and niches, is a late (and poor) figure of a woman whom the modern Pamphylians have called Bal-Kiz, the honey girl – daughter of the King of the Serpents and Queen of the Bees – after whom the modern city is named. An aqueduct ruin stalks hugely across the landscape, like one of those eighteenth-century romantically painted pictures that seem fanciful to us because we now so rarely see the objects which gave them their inspiration; it was the bridge by which this legendary king reached his beloved. Seljuk fourteenth-century pottery has been found in the theatre, evidently used in the fine days that returned to Pamphylia when trade was open and European merchants and Arab travellers visited and described the Karamanli sultans and their lands. Yet in spite of Seljuks and Byzantines, the Roman feeling remains, mixed with older feelings, and one can look from Aspendos citadel, scarcely higher than the upper gallery of the theatre below it, and easily remember how the tents of the Macedonians were encamped below, and – long before that, in 467 BC – how the Persian fleet was annihilated in the river that flowed within sight of the walls at that time, full and swift to the sea.

It is remarkable how, even in ruin, these Pamphylian towns have kept the strong diversities of their characters. Syllaeium, still rarely visited on its high precipice, pure Hellenistic, untroubled by invasion and conquered only by Time; Perge, with debased columns and slipshod walls, and mother-goddess descendant of the Neolithic or before it, the 'Lady of Perge' with her Asiatic crown, later merged with the Greek Artemis.

Antalya was a late foundation, and its little Greek came to it through Rome; but Termessus was a Pisidian city that fought Alexander, and had no Christians within its walls or at least left no churches, and wrote Greek encomiums on the pedestals of its statues, and sat in a small, most beautiful theatre high-pitched among the mountains, and looked down, three thousand feet or so, to the steep slope of the sea. There is no end to these beguiling little centres of civilization, whose intensity of life can still be felt by anyone hardy enough to battle with the thorns where most of them lie throttled. Their columns and tombs run inland along trade routes that crisscrossed Anatolia from the remoteness of Asia to the Mediterranean, where empire after empire rose and nursed the unchanging caravans and disappeared.

The colonizers of the coast were not Greeks only but Lycians, from the bay of Antalya to Caunus south of the Cnidian peninsula, a kindred people with art as lively and political machinery far more stable than that of their greater neighbour; their sporting animal-reliefs can be seen in the British Museum, where a room has at last been granted to this admirable people, whose little cities with their monuments and theatres are scattered about the hills of Xanthus (Esen Chay), and whose language, carved here and there in the aromatic valleys, can be read but not entirely understood. Pandarus came from Lycia, who was better than his later reputation would let one imagine, and very fond of horses, and Sarpedon who breached the Greek wall around the ships at Troy. And when he fell, 'as falls an oak or a silver poplar', under Patroclus' spear, Zeus called to Phoebus and bade him cleanse the black blood of battle and bear him far away, and bathe him in the streams of the river and anoint him with ambrosia, 'and clothe him in garments that wax not old, and send him to be wafted by convoy, by Sleep and Death, that quickly will set him in the rich land of Lycia.'

The Lycians are in and out all through the *Iliad*, decent brave people, friends of the Trojans; and their later history continues in this vein, for they lived together in amity, twenty-three towns in a federation of their own contriving, unique and successful until the Romans wrecked it and annexed them in AD 43. The beautiful city in the loveliest of valleys had twice been destroyed, and its inhabitants had thrown themselves into the flames rather than surrender; yet it recovered, and sent a bishop to the council of Nicaea, and in the fifth century, before subsiding under piracy and malaria, was famous for its schools.

As interesting and unique as their earliest of federations was the architecture: tombs with a columned façade, or carved to imitate timber-built houses and barns, as one can still see them on the remoter hillsides with the poplar poles that support the roof aligned end-on above the door. As the structures became elaborate, the round tree-trunks were cut to make them more symmetrical, and this line of square dentils has travelled into the classic and Renaissance and modern world, so that one can look up at some Georgian house or Palladian theatre and think of the little cities of Lycia and their quiet workmanship and honest pride.

Their land went over the passes to where Xanthus river is born, and north to Caunus, lost in marshes, and rediscovered only in the nineteenth century by someone not afraid of malaria. It was the last of the Lycian towns: and beyond that the Carian lands begin, with a people mixed beyond any disentangling – original Leleges, whatever they may have been, overlaid with some one of the many divisions of those who poured down upon the eastern Mediterranean from Caucasus or Europe in the 'great migration'. They spoke a language kindred to Greek but with words of its own – 'Carians, uncouth of speech, that possessed Miletos and the mountain of Phthires, and the streams of Maiandros and the steep crests of Mykale' (*Iliad*, II) – so that either an original difference, or an alien way of pronouncing their words, brought about the Greek invention of the word 'barbarian', which has carried through, with more than its linguistic implications, into the modern world.

It is hard on the Carians, who were an honourable fighting people, and wore a standing feather or crest in their helmets, and invented the obviously useful double hold for the inside of a shield; and became known as mercenary soldiers, particularly in the service of the Egyptians, who gave them a quarter of their own in the town of Memphis. They seem not to have been builders like their Lycian neighbours, who built them Stratoniceia where their parliaments assembled, while northern Lydian allies built Labranda, the most sacred Carian temple in the hills. Then Greece overran them, Dorians seized Halicarnassus (Bodrum) and the promontory of Cnidos, Dorian Greek became the language of the towns, Herodotus was born there, the mixed background probably helping to produce his tolerant familiarity with the diversities of nations. The temples and walls of the Carian cities became as Greek as anything in Anatolia, ranging from delicate Hellenistic in Cnidos to Diocletian's block at Stratoniceia, where the supermarket prices of his day are carved for all to see. Yet there is a difference, a roughness in Caria that distinguishes it from the mountain aristocracy of Xanthus, or from the rare and subtle elegance of Ionia. The inland towns are on the edges of small and tough plains enclosed in slabs of wooded mountains, heaps of gigantic boulders which geology seems to have been too hurried to settle into shape: Mylasa, Stratoniceia, Lagina, Alinda, Alabanda – inland places where Alexander marched with his small army on the way down from Miletus to visit the Queen of Caria, whose niece he had wished to marry when he was nineteen at his father's court. He had sent an embassy and caused no small scandal, and was now received as someone who had nearly become a member of the family, and was adopted as a son, particularly welcome at a time when the Queen was trying to fight a Persian brother-in-law on her own account and had retreated among her hillmen.

The human interest of this episode between Alexander and the Queen of Caria is of some historical importance, since it helps to explain the change in the young king during the first year of his eastern adventure – a revolution in his attitude towards the people he had come to subdue.

I have gone into it more fully in my *Alexander's Path* (London 1958), and must not linger much longer among histories and legends that crowd so thickly along every slope where the Carian mountains stretch their limbs into the western sea: Myndos and Iassos and Bargylia, and the short splendour of Halicarnassus (Bodrum), where another queen, Artemisia, defeated the Rhodian fleet out of her secret harbour and built for her Mausolus the first mausoleum to be known by that name. These queens were tough products of a matriarchal society which is known for Lycia and presumed for Caria also. The first Artemisia with Carian father and Cretan mother may be remembered as having led five ships from Halicarnassus for Xerxes, and as being the only person to advise him against fighting the Greeks by sea: 'At whom', says Herodotus, 'I do greatly marvel because, although she was a woman, she came to war against Greece; for, her husband being dead, she held the chief power, and notwithstanding she had a son that was grown up, she came to the war herself, albeit there was no need, because of her spirit and courage.' Her action in the battle itself was prompt if not sporting, for she rammed the allied King of Calynda to save herself from an enemy ship pursuing, and Xerxes seeing it thought the ship she sank was a Greek. 'All things turned to her advantage ... and this moreover, that no man was saved alive out of the ship of Calynda to be her accuser' (Herodotus, Bk VIII). The Athenians had offered a prize of 10,000 drachmae for anyone who took her alive, for 'shame that a woman should make war on Athens'; but Xerxes gave her his young sons to look after, to take them back to Ephesus. So much for the queens of Caria.

That most admirable traveller, M. Charles Texier, who gave an account of almost the whole of Asia Minor in the first half of the nineteenth century, has made a depressing list of its earthquakes from the reign of Tiberius downward, when twelve cities were swallowed in a night. Tralles (Mugla) was destroyed under Augustus, and Antioch under Trajan; Rhodes and the whole western peninsula was shaken in AD 145; 238, 244, 262, were earthquake years. In 300 it was Tyre and Sidon, in 354 Nicomedia (Izmit), Byzantium in 400, and Beirut was so levelled in 538 that what was left of the population emigrated to Sidon. In 544 an earthquake lasted for forty days and for ten in 557, and Byzantium was partly destroyed. And this has so continued down the ages, so that when I found them repairing the shaken mosque of Erzurum, I was told by a friendly engineer that 'we Turks no longer trouble to wonder whether an earthquake will happen; we are only anxious to know *where*'.

This explains the number of columns that lie prone like sausages cut into slices all over Syria and Greece and Asia Minor, and no doubt helped when one religion took to building with the properties of another, the church from the temple and the mosque from the church. Yet in spite of these frustrations of man and nature, the soil of Ionia may be said to be strewn with marble, clothed in a vesture of civilization which, however ruined, is radiant and delicate as the world has never seen again; and this belonged in a particular way to the cities of Ionia that clustered round Miletus and the temple of the twelve Ionian cities, the Panionium on the slopes of Mount Mykale, that stands above the delta of Maeander and turns its wild wooded hillsides towards Samos across a narrow arm of sea.

I made my way there in 1952, and felt and wrote about the feeling of this place, although there seemed no tangible evidence left to prove it; but many years later, travelling through Miletus, I was kindly entertained at luncheon by the German archaeologists working there, who told me that they had read my book and followed my instinct and found the temple's traces on the spot. This is not the only time that such a thing has happened, for many years before, in 1937, a friend and I went across into the Gulf to the island of Failichah, and having spent two days there trotting about its stubble fields and the small whitewashed Muslim shrine by the edge of the sea, we both felt such an atmosphere, intangible but pervasive, and thought this might perhaps be the island of Nearchus where the Macedonians watered, and asked if no carved stone or inscription had ever been found; it was only years later that a slab was dug up with a dedication to Poseidon, and the place has been excavated and identified.

Such discoveries, or rather intuitions, are the salt of travel and the riches of the inhabited world, where every creature in passing is bound to leave some little dint for ever; and the scientific traveller no doubt finds the same enjoyment on the trail of natural forces, vaster – if anything is truly smaller or greater – than the footsteps of men.

In Ionia, at any rate, these footsteps can be visibly uncovered wherever a spade is dug into a likely place, partly because the countryside is only now beginning again to be as thickly populated as it was, for instance, under the Antonines, when twenty-five million people were counted in western Anatolia alone. The wave grew and subsided, and now – after sixteen centuries – is again growing. Meanwhile what is underground has mostly been quietly left there, and what is above and happens to be near any sort of cultivation, finds its way into the peasants' lime-kilns wherever the eyes of government are turned away. But sometimes driving about inland Turkey one comes upon some solidity of stone, roughly cut out of its hillside as tomb or statue: the 'Weeping Niobe', or figures like the Hittite but outside the Hittite country, as on the way from Smyrna to Ephesus, which must most probably have been Arzawa land; or, far in the east, the splendid tombs of Amasya with their rock-cut stairways, presumed to belong to Pontic kings unnamed and unknown. These apparitions, as it were, thrusting through the crust of the classic world, which is already the world we belong to, come like geologic intrusions, making one realize the hidden life-fire that has pushed them up in its day. But when we come to Ionia, or to the age and nations which produced it, we are among our own people, separated but not really divided by that temporary darkness which drew night over Europe and hooded the Grecian dawn; and perhaps the key to the strange magic which captivated the heart of the young Alexander, and has never ceased to operate on almost every traveller, is the fact that the Dark Ages never quite settled on the eastern lands.

Miletus has been altered by geography and the caprices of the Maeander delta – so well recognized even in the days of its prosperity that law-suits could be brought against the river by the landowners settled along its banks. The earth carried down from the rich and open valley has silted the four havens, and embedded in reeds or cultivation the little island of Lade, where the Ionians in their ships fought the Persians, and lost, and the whole population of Miletus was enslaved and settled in Mesopotamia after a five years' siege. The Persians gave the hills to the Carians, and kept the plain, 'and no Milesian was left in the city of Miletus'. Yet what remains carries on the story as if the lives of men counted for nothing; the theatre of Roman Miletus dominates its landscape, and one can wander through Antonine markets and end in the quiet precincts of the mosque, a small Seljuk jewel built with precious materials that must have been lying all around.

Near by, at easy distances, the cities are spread, divided by gentle slopes that melt into one another, neither deep nor shallow but open, with the Greek characteristic of never excluding the light. Didyma is in the south above the forgotten harbour of Panormus, the patient rescue work of two generations of German archaeologists laid out on the ground around it, the oracle now bare within it, enclosed in its smooth walls. Its detail lies about as sharp as yesterday though the columns are broken; the two narrow passages that led devotees to the *cella* are there between stone sides that still have the mason's signs carved on them; and the great window looks down from its raised lintel into the denuded court. In its dilapidated death, Didyma is the living denial of all that has ever been said about the lightness and fragility of the Ionic; no weightier or more majestic peristyle of columns can ever have been waiting for their God.

One must think of the marshy Maeander plain as a shining inlet of the sea, with the port of Priene, which was given by Alexander and is now an orange plantation, lying at the city's foot, and the acropolis sheer above it; and the shores as far as the headland of Mykale so steep that when the battle of Mykale was fought (in 479 BC, on the same day as Plataea in Greece), the Spartan commander was able to sail his fleet close enough inshore for a proclamation to be made by his crier, to be heard by the colonists on land. One looks out over the plain now, to Miletus in the distance, or from the temple of Athena to the acropolis, or into the town's descending streets, across the hall with its altar, open to the kind climate, where the people sat in rows on their stone benches, disentangling as best they could their innumerable quarrels and wakening in their Greek way to heroism when the moment came.

Over the Mykale hill is Ephesus – with tourism reborn on its shores, and Diana of the Ephesians rediscovered, and the debased ages made visible in stone. The perennial character of a religion that gives dividends goes on from century to century: the straight paved street of Rome is followed by the Byzantine avenue of Arcadius, the columns are taken to live again, immortal, under the dome of St Sophia, the tomb of St John trails neglected until the Christians of Ohio now rebuild him, while the Seljuk mosque, where the old stones were used, stands smooth and mellow with centuries of sunshine inside it on the slope of the hill.

Towns, remembered or forgotten, each with liberties that were ancient and became municipal under Rome, follow the rivers and fountains, wherever there was water to live: Magnesia on Maeander, Heraklea of the great walls, Belevi, Nysa, Aphrodisias where stadium and theatre are now uncovered, and northward to the un-Ionic steepness of Pergamon and Hellenistic walls and later fancies, a continuous movement as if stone were alive.

The delicate perfection of Ionia disappears as one leaves the Maeander and reaches other rivers – Lycus below Hierapolis or Hermus and Pactolus at Sardis. The great blocks of theatre and scattered tombs of Hierapolis (Pamukkale) are Roman, though its petrified white waterfalls must have been a centre of fear and worship from the earliest times. Eunuchs were said to be the only human beings who could avoid asphyxiation while bending over the Plutonium – a hole in the ground which has never been located but was said to kill an ox if it entered: the eunuchs are suggested by Strabo to have solved the problem by simply holding their breath. The warm volcanic water now lies transparent over pale fallen columns, and not the waterfalls only but the whole landscape looked petrified, strange and sterile when I went there – now brought up to date by a hotel, I am told.

Sardis had gentler gods, and Pactolus tumbling between golden poplars from Tmolus flows beside it where the hills meet the plain of Hermus. The elegance of Didyma is absent, yet there is no great step between Greek and Lydian in columns or decoration – the familiar egg pattern, with a barbarian touch! As we climb to the Anatolian plateau, we are back in lands which Greek and Roman civilizations penetrated and moulded but never quite transformed, the far-away world of central Asia and its caravans, of the great migrations unsoftened by the Mediterranean, of the trade which, creeping at its walking pace across the plains and ranges, enriched dynasty after dynasty, nation after nation.

When the Hittites moved south before finally disappearing, the Phrygians stepped in from the Thracian north through a chaos of warfare – and grew strong in the country that stretches from Ankara to the Sangarius (Sakarya). Priam as a young man came from Troy to help them against the Amazons: 'Erewhile fared I to Phrygia, the land of vines, and there saw I that the men of Phrygia, they of the nimble steeds, were very many ... encamped along the banks of Sangarius' (*Iliad*, III). They were horsemen, and fought from chariots like all the Thracians and Maonians from Tmolus and Sardis their neighbours; and even today, if one goes to their legendary centre, across plains that were so nearly fatal to the Crusaders, through pastoral valleys and small streams to the tangle of rocks where they built what has come down to us as the tomb of Midas – an ugly but interesting monument unlike any other – even now one may see the country carts trotting by with a cluster of foals and ponies round them running free.

A surprising amount of intercourse across the Anatolian plateau is revealed by the lists in the *Iliad* and the number of visits paid; a good deal of intercourse, too, between Greece and Anatolia, shown incidentally by Paris's young man's tour. Legendary as regards Bellerophon or the travelling philosopher Mopsus, it is well attested in the life of Alexander, whose friend and private seer, Aristander, came from Lycia and spent many years at the Macedonian court. The Cretan and Cycladic and Mycenaean fashion travelled for centuries round the bays of Anatolia before Troy was destroyed, and most of the places where their painted pottery has been discovered had been trading stations, settled on low promontories as we have noted, before the Ionians came; but Miletus was an actual colony of Cretans named after the Cretan Miletus, and over sixty settlements had spread from her along the northern and western coasts when the Lydians followed the Hittites and Phrygians as the main Anatolian power. They used the imperial roads and developed the use of money, shepherding the Asiatic traffic across the Anatolian plateau to the Grecian coasts. And when they had fallen, defeated by Cyrus, and Miletus with the other Ionians had revolted, and the Persians destroyed her, the later wave of Grecian settlers were already firmly established, too useful to the continental Persians to be lightly oppressed or dislodged.

Two centuries passed, and the Macedonian armies marched from Gordium, reached inland cities of Syria and Egypt, and left their names and memories scattered through Central Asia to Bactria and Samarkand and the Indus. It was not until they reached the eastern marches that the Greek genius found the equally strong civilization of Persia on its way. When the Romans came, little over a century later, they brought a second wave of Greek influence with them, and in the course of the next five hundred years spread a fairly uniform surface over Anatolia, so that even the wild Pisidians could be visited (by an apostle), and – in the second century AD – could spread their fashion of sarcophagus (Sidamaran) across the Roman world.

The distributing centre in this early world of commerce was Troy. When the war of the *Iliad* opened, the Black Sea was one of the main sources of the Mediterranean for the new age of iron, with open mines for both iron and copper (still worked today in the south coast hills), and gold in the far north of the Altai, and corn that – before north Africa came to be exploited – was the defence against famine for all the sterile headlands and islands whose populations outran their supplies. If the corn through the Bosphorus failed, the only resource left to them – to limit their numbers – was exposure of female infants at birth (not difficult in the stony wilderness that climbs up behind every Greek townlet on its bay). In this light one may look into the economic background of the *Iliad*, and see the city of Priam astride, like the later Byzantium, on the main gates of the main necessities of its age – a situation both invidious and rich ('Of old time all mortal men would tell of this city of Priam for the much gold and bronze thereof...').

The importance of Troy as a gateway may be measured by the debris of its other eight cities that rose and sank unsung. And the early days passed, and Agamemnon lay with only the hum of bees in the shadow of his tomb, and the black-prowed ships landed their later colonists among the thinly scattered Leleges of Anatolia, and made friends of the Lydian successors to the Phrygians. The caravans with the chain of their journeys behind them unloaded and loaded on open beaches – the wooden holds filling, as one can still see them here and there, along slim, precarious gangways where the sheep file in or the amphorae are lifted, handiwork of Cnidos, or Telos, or Clazomenae, baked red earth stamped with their seal. When the unending trade of Asia enriched them, and temples and quays and public buildings lined the shores with marble, the great cities of Marmara or the Black Sea coast, colonies of Miletus (Cyzicus, Heraklea, Sinope) or of Megara (Trebizond, Chalcedon, Byzantium), grew strong enough to favour or resist Mithridates or Rome. Troy became history, so that the chief vestiges of its great climax were destroyed; the *Iliad* remained alone as monument and guide, to lead Heinrich Schliemann eighteen centuries later to his discovery of the site.

But the gateway of the Black Sea remained, and Byzantium – a late-comer among the colonists – held the keys. The importance of the site was unaltered. Polybius, writing over a thousand years after the siege of Troy, could remark that the Greeks 'would lose all this commerce' if the Byzantines were unfriendly.

49   Part of the Hellenistic frieze from the north wall of the adyton at Didyma.

50   Side of a third-century sarcophagus of Sidamara type in the Konya Archaeological Museum, depicting the labours of Hercules: the Nemean lion, the Hydra of Lerna, the Erymanthian boar, the Arcadian stag, the birds of the Stymphalian lake. These columned sarcophagi were invented in the little city of Sidamara on the uplands of Pisidia, and came to be known by this name.

51, 52   Some 40 miles east of Antalya are the substantial remains of the Pamphylian town and port of Side, founded – according to Strabo – by Cyme in Aeolis (on the western coast of Asia Minor), perhaps in the seventh century BC. Alexander the Great came here, and in 190 BC a Roman fleet supported by the Rhodians defeated that of Antiochus III under Hannibal in spite of help from Side. The importance of the town lay in its maritime prestige, not in the major happenings of history. That it flourished in Hellenistic and Roman times is evident from the grand scale of its aqueduct, streets and public buildings, its two ports and its impressive theatre, which stands in the middle of the town. In the absence of any hillside, it is built up entirely on subvaults like a Roman amphitheatre. Its capacity is calculated to have been 13,000 persons (nearly twice the capacity of the theatre at Aspendos), an eloquent testimony to the size of the population whose centre was Side in Roman times. The ornate sculpture of the *scenae frons* now lies in chaos on the stage and *orchestra*. Plate 52 shows a fragment containing a bust in a roundel.

53, 54   Aspendos (Balkiz) was a Greek city colonized from Argos in the seventh century BC. It is likely, since the name is not Greek, that in fact these colonizers took over an earlier settlement, and indeed there is a tradition that, after the Trojan War, Achaeans came to southeast Asia Minor and founded the earliest colonies. The city was well-placed on the Eurymedon – once a navigable river – where Kimon of Athens won a decisive victory against the Persians in 468 BC. Situated on two easily defensible hills and in a temperate climate, Aspendos was a commercial port and a naval base in its heyday, and was besieged by Alexander the Great when he marched across Pamphylia.

On the flat top of the larger hill are the remains of the agora, with shops and nymphaeum and other buildings; beyond it the arches of a fine Roman aqueduct stalk across a village of small huts. The chief monument is the theatre, built on the eastern slope of the smaller hill – the best-preserved Roman theatre known. Inscriptions show it to have been dedicated to the local gods and to the family of Antoninus Pius. The stage is very large, backed by a wall 120 yards long and 80 feet high, pierced by three doors and decorated with two storeys of columns, entablatures and pediments.

55   Priene, modern Gülbahçe, about 60 miles south of Izmir, can now be reached by a good road from Söke (12 miles). It was the smallest of the twelve cities of the Ionian League and caretaker of the track across Mykale that led to their common temple, the Panionium. The battle of Mykale, which liberated Ionia from Persian rule, was fought close by, some four miles west along the coast, on the same day as the Greek victory at Plataea, in 479 BC. The city, which had been destroyed when first the Persians came and the Lydian empire was defeated, now flourished and rebuilt itself in the fourth century BC on the Hellenistic grid-plan invented by the architect Hippodamus of Miletus. Alexander the Great gave it a new port, which has silted up and is now an orange grove, and helped in the building of the fine Ionic temple to Athena designed by Pytheos, with

eleven columns on the longer and six on the shorter side. Five of the columns (seen here) have recently been re-erected.

Most of the troubles of Priene came to it from the restlessness of the River Maeander weaving from side to side in its wide plain, and bringing down thousands of cubic feet of mud, leading to successive re-foundations of the city on different sites. The receding sea slowly drained away the character of a sea-port from the city and left it to its quiet perfection: a bishopric in early Christian days and then silence – until the German archaeologists began to open out its lovely ruins to the sun.

56   Miletus, now Balat, in the district of Söke, was the chief city of the Ionian League – 'the town of a twelve-walled people that is chief among the Achaeans' (Timotheus, fourth century BC). It was a colony of Cretans who gave it the name of Miletus and handed on their Mycenean pottery forms to later colonizers. The sea has left its four harbours, and the island of Lade is now almost six miles inland, where the naval battle with the Persians was fought and the splendour of Miletus destroyed (494 BC). It revived under Rome, and its greatest surviving monument is the theatre, with a stage 110 feet long and built in the second and third centuries AD to hold 25,000 spectators.

57–58   Below Didyma, one of the best beaches in all Turkey: an almost land-locked, delightful sea and a comfortable motel.

59, 60   Didyma: ruins of the Temple of Apollo. The Apollo of Didyma, otherwise Branchidae (from Branchus, son of Apollo), owned this oldest and most famous among the sanctuaries and oracles of the Ionian world. The Sacred Way leading up to it from the harbour of Panormus was lined with archaic statues, many of which are now in the British Museum. The temple was burnt by Darius, and its statue carried to Ecbatana; and the oracle remained silent until the coming of Alexander, when it wisely foretold his victory and gained funds for the rebuilding. Strabo calls it the largest temple in the world, too vast to be roofed; as it now stands, it is one of the most beautiful of Hellenistic ruins, and the most splendid known in the Ionic order. The great window where the oracles were proclaimed is intact, and so are the dark and narrow passages that lead to the *cella* below; along its walls the delicate pilasters remain.

61, 62, 63   Perge is another very ancient Pamphilian town that continued to flourish through the Hellenistic age and under the Romans, whose brutal robberies of its works of art are recorded by Cicero. The Artemis of

Perge was succeeded by the preaching of St Paul, the smooth and delicate finish of the Hellenistic walls by the functional Roman, and the columns blossomed into their late and elaborate Corinthian capitals. Ten thousand people sat in its theatre, and its stadium measured 760 × 114 feet. The magic of the Hellenistic has coarsened to the Roman, but much remains, and one can wander up the once-colonnaded street of Perge, and see in one's mind's eye the water running in its marble conduit down the middle, the shops on either side, and baths and gymnasium below the more ancient acropolis above. The photographs show a fragmentary Roman relief, the masonry of one of the walls, and a surviving Corinthian column.

64, 65   Termessus, in spite of its long age under Rome, has remained a chiefly Hellenistic town: the beautiful building of the agora and the absence of any sign of a Christian church within its walls strengthen this impression, and the place itself still breathes the toughness of its Pisidian mountaineers. Alexander, with his eye for what was feasible, gave up the siege. After his death, the brother of his friend Perdiccas took refuge here, and the young men of the city fought for him against Antigonus's forty thousand men and refused to give him up. Their more prudent parents and elders betrayed him, choosing a moment when the young warriors were away; his monument carved on the rocky hillside, with horse and shield, could be admired until a few years ago, when the peasants smashed the shield hoping for hidden gold. Enough remains in the town to show it to have been rich and beautiful, and the theatre in particular is enhanced by its position – looking 3,000 feet down to the sea. From the necropolis at the hilltop a splendid view shows Tahtali Dagh in the south-west, and the hills that stretch away to the Chelidonian cape, the first frontier of Rome in Asia Minor.

66, 67, 68   Hierapolis (Pamukkale) is 14 miles north of Denizli, on a limestone plateau 325 feet above the Çuruksu plain. Here the natural hot springs have provided bathing and medical establishments for age upon age: the calcareous stream has poured itself over the plateau's edge, building pillars and cornices and basins out of its own substance, white and powdery as salt; and on the flatness of the plateau the ancient waters still feed a transparent pool whose floor is pale with fallen marble columns.

The Plutonium, where the gods of the nether world were worshipped, is now a mere ditch and has lost the opening which would kill a bull but was apparently innocuous to eunuchs. Strabo threw sparrows in, that immediately died.

A hotel has been built recently, close to the huge marble-floored arcades of the Roman gymnasium. Inland are the theatre and the necropolis, tumbled with every variety of tombstone.

69, 70, 71 Aphrodisias (Geyre), 40 miles south from Nazilli in the Maeander valley. It was made a free city in 39 BC, and continued prosperous and famous for the working of its native marble throughout the Imperial age of Rome, and – under a new name of Stauropolis – into the Byzantine age. The coming of the Seljuks, and finally the sack by Tamerlane in 1402, caused it to be gradually forgotten, with few delicate fluted columns left to stand against the background of Mount Cadmus (Honaz Dagh); until first the Italians and then the Americans dug out the 735-foot-long stadium and the second-century odeon on the edge of its ancient square. Statues, friezes, capitals, columns and tombs are heaped in the half-light of a barn now used as a temporary museum, where the contrast makes Time visible, as it were, to those tourists who make their easy journeys along the new asphalt road.

72 Ephesus (Selçuk), 44 miles south from Izmir by road or rail. Founded it was said by the Amazons, Ephesus continued to flourish as a Greek city long after the temple of Artemis (one of the seven wonders of the world), which had made its fame, had been destroyed. Justinian built the gate that leads on the high ground to the church of St John (now being restored). He carried away the temple's ancient columns, and the Seljuk Turks left their name to the city. The famous temple has vanished in a marshy hollow, and its stones no doubt helped to build the church which, in its turn, supplied the beautiful yellow stone of the Seljuk mosque: the three faiths stand embodied in the landscape, one above the other on their hill.

Shown here is the Arcadian Way (so-called from the emperor Arcadius, who restored it at the end of the fourth century AD), which runs for almost a third of a mile between the theatre and the port. Its width of 36 feet was paved with slabs of marble, under which ran the drains of the town. Lined with statues, it was illuminated at night – a splendid piece of town planning, finished at the very moment when the Goths were about to sack Rome in 410.

73 The Artemis of Ephesus. The Sacred Way, from the city of Ephesus to the temple, was discovered only in the 1870s. It is now being followed step by step by Austrian archaeologists, who are laying bare the rich, luxurious city on either side, and came upon Artemis herself (now in the museum at Ephesus), dressed in the symbols of fertility and standing between two stags. The many ovoids that look like a multitude of breasts are, we are told, eggs, evidently here regarded as a gift from the gods.

74, 75 Sardis, some 65 miles east of Izmir, was the home of the Lydians, the people whose language is said to have given us the word 'tyrant'. As far as one can see, they were less tyrannical than many others, and kept their solicitude for the trade route which brought their wealth, and along which they were the first to invent and use coined money. Their king, Croesus, became synonymous with riches. When, in 546 BC, he was defeated and slain by the Persians, Sardis became the western focus of the Persians' vast empire, and the trade route became the Royal Road, linking Persia with the Mediterranean.

The principal building now visible is the Hellenistic marble temple of Artemis, one of the largest Ionic temples in the Greek world. Like the Doric Parthenon at Athens, it was fronted by eight columns, and it was flanked on each side by no fewer than twenty. The better-preserved columns are Roman replacements; the temple suffered severely from earthquake in AD 17 and from flood in the third century. Plate 75 shows a detail of one of the Ionic capitals, a highly original design with a six-petalled flower between the volutes and a row of egg-and-dart ornament forming the bottom of the abacus.

76, 77, 78, 79, 80 Pergamon is another very ancient site, and her early lords are said to have drawn their descent from the nymph Callisto, whom Zeus lifted to heaven in the shape of the Great Bear. Long after this, however, the city on its high hill gave a lodging to Xenophon and his Ten Thousand, and is recorded in his history. She came to her greatest fame and prosperity under the Attalids, who were lucky enough to have in their safe-keeping the wealth of Lysimachus – one of the Diadochi after Alexander, when he was vanquished and killed. The Attalid was a popular and civilized dynasty, and the atmosphere of Pergamon is Hellenistic in spite of the centuries of Roman rule. In AD 133 the reigning Attalid handed it as a gift to Rome, then in her fifty-third year in Asia Minor. It was by then famous for its art, its library, its commerce and manufactures – particularly the parchment, *pergamena*, to which it gave its name.

The theatre (pl. 76) was finished in its present form in the early third century AD, in the reign of Caracalla, and could hold 50,000 spectators.

The Asclepeion (pl. 77), a very large complex at the foot of the hill, was not only a cult centre but a sort of health resort to which invalids would come in hope of a cure. The treatment was more psychological than physical, including suggestion, dream interpretation, bathing, sun-bathing, and theatrical entertainments.

The Museum contains works from every period of Pergamon's history. Plate 78: detail of a Hellenistic Aphrodite, with the hand of a vanished cupid still pressed against her leg. Plate 79: a small winged victory, part of the roof-ornament of a temple. Plate 80: the three-headed dog Cerberus, so unlike the tempestuous style of most Pergamene sculpture that it must surely be an import.

81, 82   Amasya, the oldest Pontic capital, overlooked by precipice-cut tombs of early unnamed kings, is still an important town on the Green River (the Yeshil Irmak). This flows between cliffs so close together that one might call them a gorge, and the town's picturesque wooden houses are dwarfed by the giant crags behind them. High up above is the castle, with ruinous towers and Byzantine walls, as well as later additions: for all rulers in turn have held to the stronghold. A number of beautiful Seljuk buildings are here in good repair, and the list of fine mosques closes with that of Ottoman Beyazit, its cloistral library still useful beside it. The most interesting finds of recent years in Amasya are the skeletons of some of the Timurid rulers, which can be seen in quiet vaults cut into the rock at the foot of the acropolis.

83–84, 85   The site of Troy is about 19 miles from Çanakkale on the Dardanelles, along a good road to Ayvalik on the Aegean. Its first impression may be a disappointment to anyone who has not recently read his *Iliad*: the zeal of Augustus, anxious to flatten the acropolis for the building of his temple, razed away much of the Homeric city, and the whole slope is a palimpsest of nine successive layers that mark its history. Schliemann's identification of the second city has been discarded, and the sixth is held to have been the stronghold of Priam towards the end of the thirteenth century BC. Strips of the pavement are shown where Helen walked, but such tangible reminders are not essential: the geography is recognizable and unaltered. The reedy flats are there, with the sea beyond them and nothing to impede the gallop of the Lycian horses towards the rampart and the black-prowed ships. The plain holds the two rivers and their meeting, and even the oak trees are still scattered here and there. And far behind us, above the wooded outlines of Ida, one can, in favourable weather, get the sharp and now uninhabited summit that was the throne of Zeus.

61

62 63

66

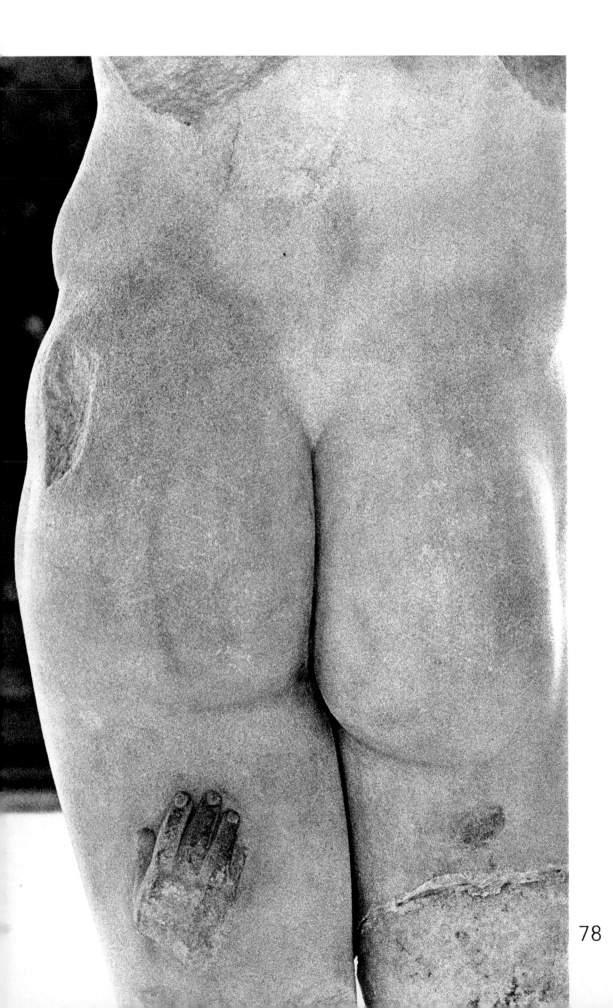

4 The Byzantines

We have watched the earliest community yet known in Turkey telling its story long before the written word was discovered; and have then followed later traces of Greek or kindred peoples round contours of coasts and up rivers, by steps clearly marked in unsurpassed beauty of ruins, through the early colonial and the Hellenistic into the Roman age.

These Greek traces, however slight, are bright with a definite light – a sharpness of outline that belongs to the Hellenic influence wherever it touches, and is helped by a self-sufficient tradition, believed in and carefully preserved, which showed no sign of any wish to sink and lose itself in any other background, either along the coastal lands of Anatolia or in the great trading cities where the successors of Alexander had done their best to preserve a pure and unadulterated Hellenic stream. With the spread of Rome, and the coming of Italians who have always been easy mixers, the situation changed into that alternation of familiarity and massacre which has given such frequent shocks to Latin colonization. But even so, the outlines lost little of their sharpness: even along the eastern marches, where the Persian civilization gradually took over and the Greek remained isolated – in urban islands separated one from the other by long days' journeys along the thread of trade – even among these outposts that stretched to Alexander's farthest horizon of the Indus and beyond it, the Greek clarity remained, recognizable if not intact. The language spoken in the latest city discovered on the Oxus (modern Amu Darya) remained during the two centuries of its existence as classic and elegant as it was at its foundation; the Greek coins of Bactria are among the finest of Greek coins; the cities of Mesopotamia under the Parthians remained intrinsically Greek.

At the end of the third century AD, Diocletian transported the centre of empire from Rome to Nicomedia (modern Izmit). This process had, as a matter of fact, been for quite a long time on the way. A few years later, on 11 May 330, Constantine inaugurated the new eastern capital at Byzantium, after hesitating between Nish, his own birthplace, and Troy. The city which had begun rather late in the Greek colonizing race as a settlement from Megara, now took the Emperor's name, Constantinople, and might have been expected to settle into the mould that had long become familiar to Greek Mediterranean towns. The Black Sea queens, Heraklea or Cyzicus or Sinope, or the intellectual and trading capitals of Antioch and Alexandria in the south, might have expected a city to join them possibly greater than, but not basically different from, themselves. The extraordinary uniqueness of the Byzantine could not have been foretold.

The geographic position on the Bosphorus helped. It was the most fortunate that could be imagined, both for defence and for trade: the Black Sea was still the gateway for grain, fish and iron, basic needs with which the eastern Mediterranean was poorly provided; and the site of Byzantium on its promontory was still, as Polybius had observed it five hundred years before, 'more favourable to security ... than that of any city in the world known to us' (Pol., IV, 38). But these advantages were not enough in themselves, and were shared, though in a lesser degree, by many an acropolis along the Anatolian shores: a more particular ingredient was required to plant Constantinople mystically in the hearts of men.

This was provided by the Christian religion, and very few single acts in history have been more influential than Constantine's decision to adopt it when he did. Young, starry-eyed and uncorrupted, it stepped from the terror of the Diocletian persecutions into the heart of power, still swathed like a chrysalis in those Platonic vestments that bound it to the civilized world from which it came. For a short time – a very short time between the third and fifth centuries AD – the Fathers of the eastern church speak with the tongues of angels; the wildernesses of Cappadocia blossom with a delicacy and a joy which were never captured in the west; and in this transient flowering of deliverance and emotion the enduring character of the Byzantine was hammered out of Time.

One cannot understand it unless one has some acquaintance with these words 'first spoken beside remote rivers and in long-vanished churches' that still affect our lives and were long afterwards rediscovered and quoted by John Donne or Thomas Aquinas, so that they have entered into the spiritual treasury of the west. They were mostly packed into a single generation that followed the Alexandrian precursors and produced Gregory of Nyssa, Gregory of Nazianzus, Basil, John Cantacuzene, John Damascene. Nearly contemporaries, they had all met terror and famine and bloodshed in their turn, yet the sense of guilt, so dismal in the west, does not touch them: 'Men have been endowed with immortality; let them seize their endowment; let them walk the earth for a little space as though they were in Heaven.' So writes Clement of Alexandria, and adds that 'all this life is a holy festival'. They felt the sanctity indwelling in all things, and the extraordinary dignity of the human state, making of man a living image 'partaking with the Godhead both in rank and in name, ... reposing in the blessedness of immortality, ... a perfect likeness to the beauty of the Godhead in all that belongs to the dignity of majesty' (Clement of Alexandria). In his essays on civilization, Lord Clark describes the Renaissance as discovering the dignity of man; in the same way one may say that the Byzantine discovered his divinity.

The world is not easy for mystics, and by AD 325, the bishops were already quarrelling at the council of Nicaea. Yet with all its imperfections, the atmosphere of those first centuries had been built into the resurrected city and remained, although the links with the older world, only gradually broken, left many things intact. Constantine himself was baptised only just before his death (337), and no one has ever been quite able to probe the quality of his conversion; and for a century and a half, though the Roman habit of raising the elected emperor on the soldiers' shields was soon discontinued, his election and proclamation remained with the armies, while the people never gave up their own ultimate right of choice.

The steps were easier than one might suppose between Neo-Platonic paganism and the new dispensation. The deification of kings was familiar in the east through Persia, and had been found politically useful not only by Alexander and his successors but by Roman emperors such as Aurelian; it made no great outward change to become vicar of the Godhead upon earth. In the gradual step-over, the sceptre of Zeus was transformed and adopted; the ritual of approach (Diocletian first made courtiers stand in his presence) was taken up and elaborated; and the scarlet boots embroidered with golden eagles which Diocletian had worn as a demi-god were of the same pattern as those by which, it is said, the last of the Byzantine emperors was recognized in 1453 under the walls of Theodosius, among the heaps of the slain. The emperor and his court still looked Roman enough in the Hippodrome, at whose inaugural ceremony in Constantinople the statue of Apollo, transformed into a likeness of Constantine, had been carried by legionaries dressed equally for Christian or for pagan holiness in white. The churches of St Irene and of the Apostles were not founded for another seven years, and St Sophia – to be twice burned down before Justinian's final building – was first opened thirty years after the new Rome's dedication to the Holy Trinity and the Mother of God.

One must remember that the East alone has shown itself able to reconcile an actively spiritual government with the temporal climates of everyday life: the capacity has come down into modern times, and theocracy was normal until recently in the Yemen, for instance. It was implicit among the Hebrews, and intrinsic to the mystique of Persia both before and after the Muslim conquest, and still illustrates the basic difference between Sunni and Shi'a in the Islamic world. However cautious in his steps, Constantine was firm in his theocratic attitude; he was, and intended to remain, regent of his church on earth. Although a popular right of election, and indeed of rebellion, persisted throughout the 1100 years that were to follow – a latent safeguard for times of trouble – the imperial throne remained firmly founded in a spiritual world. Unity of religion, far more than territory, should be regarded as defining the Byzantine sphere: the mosaics of Palermo, Ravenna, Salonica, the Vladimir Virgin, and the Balkan churches are all Byzantium, though outside the later territorial girdle. The nails of the Cross, discovered by that indefatigable archaeologist St Helena, were melted, it is said, into the head of the Constantine-Apollo statue, and are not inapt as symbols for a government that intended to be Christ's under the lineaments of empire; whose earthly head could enter the Holy of Holies and consider himself the thirteenth among the apostles, and wear a dress of resurrection at Easter, and dine with twelve guests at his table, and sleep under a cross of green mosaic in his palace on the Marmara shore.

As the generations passed – through 1124 years, to the fall of the city – the splendour of this status became ever more hieratic and more enshrined, until the later incumbents tended to escape from the confinement of the main palace with its churches, halls and gardens, its combination of ritual and business (the government silk-weaving monopoly was established within the palace walls). After the twelfth century, they built themselves the palace of Blachernae above the western end of the Golden Horn, whence one could enjoy a day's hunting in open country. War itself must have been a relief from the weight of bureaucracy, and most of the emperors were personal leaders in the field.

The stability of their government, in spite of a number of storms and several revolutions that rocked it, was not maintained exclusively by divine intervention: a remarkably efficient civil service was its backbone. There was no poison of nationalism in a society based mainly on wealth; religious orthodoxy and not racialism caused such trouble as from time to time occurred. Until the later centuries – when the Latin powers grew too overwhelming and Venetians or Genoese swept the Byzantine commercial navies off their own seas – the road was free for all, with no particular prejudice against any one of the many races spread along Mediterranean or Aegean and across the Armenians to the Persian border, or north across the Black Sea to the Russian and Bulgarian steppes.

This wide tolerance allowed the most acute among the business peoples of the Levant to spread their wings and make their fortunes, and often to steer the state. Democracy included royal marriages, for the emperors' brides were chosen for their personal gifts of beauty or intelligence apart from any prerogative of birth; and there was no prejudice against the sending of some young member of the imperial family to marry and slowly civilize the Russian, Bulgarian, or even western wildness. One of the most pleasing interludes in Ibn Batuta's account of his fourteenth-century travels is the record of his journey in the suite of a Christian princess visiting her father in Constantinople from her new home in the Mongol court of the Steppes. The Byzantine women were remarkably free and influential, and even slavery, though generally practised, was disapproved of when the slaves were Christians; there were more protests against it in Constantinople than around the well-stocked markets of Venice or of Florence.

Eunuchs enjoyed a status of almost unparalleled favour. The fact that they could have no children made them safe, and there was no question of their inheriting the throne; so that the personal service of the court became their particular province, and in the tenth century they rose to the height of their power, to become high chamberlain, chief minister of empire, or vizier. Such things drift into a country from its neighbours – Persia in this instance – and continue in the same sort of surroundings from one pattern of civilization to another. The respectability of the eunuch's situation comes down in my mind almost to modern times in a strange little story told me by a member of one of the Turkish families in Cairo, in whose grandmother's house it occurred in the days of the sultan Abdul Hamit.

At that time, small girl-children could be bought in Istanbul and treated kindly as daughters in some speculating family, until, at fourteen or so, if they were beautiful they could be sold at a profit. A child to whom this happened, when the time came, having been called in by her supposed mother to be looked at by two female visitors, was told to prepare for her wedding and was carried off in a closed carriage to a house at the far end of the town. Beautifully dressed, she was surprised to find no signs of festivity and no one about except one little weeping Negro girl. After some hours they were each handed a passport, and as night fell were bundled onto a ship and sent to Alexandria and thence Cairo. No sooner had they rested there, than the major-domo in my friend's grandmother's house appeared, and instantly bought the girl, who soon became the old lady's personal maid. She was kindly treated and much liked by my informer and by all the young women of the household, and when her mistress would sometimes visit Istanbul and be invited as a relative to a private interview by the Sultan, the young maid would wait in an anteroom, where the chief of the eunuchs saw, liked, and proposed to marry her. In the course of time and after some apparently very contented years, the poor man was had up for embezzlement and hanged at the end of Galata Bridge. Nor does the story end there; for his successor noticed the widow, thought her (and her matrimonial moderation possibly) desirable, married her in his turn, and gave her a prosperous and contented old age. It is, in its modern dress, still a Byzantine story and shows slavery in its kindest and not unusual light. The grimmer record is the historic fact that a large proportion of the Bosphorus shipping, first Byzantine and then later Italian, carried slaves from Russia or Bulgaria to Europe, paying some ten per cent duty on the way.

Ten per cent was the fixed rate for goods either coming or going between the Bosphorus and the Dardanelles, and one must remember that although the singularity of the Byzantine edifice was produced by its religion, its security was peculiarly financial. It depended on the great east-west routes of Asia, most of which led through Persian land. In spite of this drawback, two-thirds of the world's riches were said by the Greeks to be within the city walls, and when, in 1204, Constantinople was sacked by the Crusaders, the French booty alone amounted to seven times the annual revenue of England.

The sixth century reached the high-water mark of this trade, and the Silk Road, which skirted the Gobi and led south of the Tien Shan from China through Balkh or Samarkand, brought the most precious of all the Byzantine raw materials across the Euphrates, by way of Nisibis (Nusaybin) or Dara, whose ruins now mark the deserty Turkish frontier of the south, and thence across Anatolia to the capital. The frontier dues diminished the profits, and any disturbance such as Hunnish raids beyond the far Pamirs would shake the markets of the west, so that the Russian steppes continued to be explored and incidentally civilized in an attempt to find a cheaper way and circumvent the Persians. The only other route not interfered with by them came up through the Red Sea or Persian Gulf, and was in the hands of Abyssinian or Syrian traders and soon to be shut off by the Arab conquests of the seventh century. Before this happened, two monks by a fortunate coincidence had brought the eggs and the secret of the silkworms in a hollow bamboo from China, and Justinian's factory in the gardens of Marmara continued to produce brocades which for many centuries were to be the most prized materials known to the west. They can be seen in the robes of Charlemagne in Vienna, and the Ottomans continued the tradition; and about forty years ago the Christian women of Baghdad and Damascus still went to their churches wrapped in hand-woven bright colours that had come down to them through their forbears, striped with gold.

Over and over again through its ages, Constantinople is described as the most splendid and richest of cities, rich in churches and relics and gold – a combination of Mecca and Paris to the barbarian. The palace of Blachernae, when the Second Crusade in the twelfth century passed by, is admired, ornamented with marbles and mosaics and gardens, a triangle overlooking the Golden Horn and the city and the open country beyond the majestic walls. The town appeared squalid and dark to the Crusaders, but one may say that Arab travellers were liable to get exactly the same impression from the narrow dirty ways of western towns. These contrasts did not distress the Byzantines: their aqueducts and the width of their streets and the size of their windows were regulated by government, and the people were anyway much more interested in theology than in drains. Their revolutions were practically always based on religion; and one of the noticeable shocks given them by the emperor Andronicus – who came to a bad end – was his protest against theology as the only and everlasting subject of conversation at meal-times.

The great Puritan split over images and their worship was typically Byzantine and dislocated the realm for the whole of the eighth century. A more fatal disagreement, over the single or dual nature of Christ, had been instrumental in losing them their southern lands a century before, when the Arab conquerors found Egyptians, Palestinians and Syrians already inclined towards them. A great variety of deadlocks were bound to appear in a state whose head considered himself the personal representative of God and the preserver of orthodoxy as well (a task which the Almighty himself seems to have given up from the very beginning). Ecclesiastical detail is not for an essay, nor can one deal so shortly with the extremely personal characters of the emperors through the 1124 years of their story. What I should like briefly to do is to look at these centuries not in their well-known splendour, but in the hard light of their task: their brave, prolonged and efficient defence of the civilized Christian-classic world against the waves of east and west that finally submerged it. Out of the long, heroic saga one can pick out, I think, four turning-points, each one contributing in its own particular field to the ultimate catastrophe.

The Loss of the South

The first and least obvious among these tragic milestones was Justinian's reconquest of the Roman Mediterranean in the sixth century AD. 'We have good hopes', the Emperor had proclaimed, 'that God will grant us to restore our authority over the remaining countries which the ancient Romans possessed to the limits of both oceans' (J.B. Bury, *A History of the Later Roman Empire*, London 1923, II.26). He very nearly succeeded, at a cost which left most of what had been the ancient world in ruins. The appalling picture drawn by Procopius, and others, was not entirely Justinian's doing, but there is no doubt that a great part of it was due to his successful wars and their taxes. The plague in AD 543 added its dead. The frontier fortresses so lavishly built were in little over a generation in ruins; the cities had to economize, 'nor were the public lamps kept burning ... nor was there any other consolation ... for theatres and hippodromes, and circuses were closed ... and there was no laughter in life' (Proc., *Anec.* XXVI.7.10). The discontent aroused added its virus to the great controversy of the single or dual nature of Christ, on which the Emperor – anxious to keep on terms with his newly reinstated West – was for compromise, while the more realistic Empress Theodora recognized the danger and fanaticism of the Egyptians and Syrians, and kept a Monophysite patriarch and many of his bishops hidden from persecution for years in one of her palaces on the Marmara shore. While the streets of Alexandria ran with blood, the government on the Bosphorus came to be detested; and when the Muslim armies whirled like an apocalypse out of the desert, many cities such as Damascus welcomed the invaders and got their bishops or leading citizens to arrange a surrender with the Arabian treasurer, Mansur.

The loss of these southern provinces was disastrous, since they included the terminals of the Spice Road, which now became a highway for purely Arabian commerce and soon dealt with Europe direct. Aleppo rose while Antioch declined, and the young and adventurous Arabians took to the sea. Tarsus and the Taurus range behind it became the borderland against Anatolia, the strong-point of a fluctuating frontier that was to divide the ancient Roman world as it had never been divided before. From the east Persian border to Morocco, 'there was no city of importance but had in Tarsus a house for its citizens where its warriors lived. Once they arrived, they settled down in garrison. They received rich and plentiful arms from the funds sent to them by the sultans and wealthy men who gave voluntary aid. There was hardly a chief or a distinguished man of the countries mentioned but endowed for them farms or inns.' (Aly Muhammad Fahmy, *Muslim Sea-Power in the East Mediterranean*, London 1950.)

By the beginning of the tenth century, Tarsus and its fleet had become the terror of the Aegean. The north African coast was Muslim, with an arsenal at Tunis and a naval base in Cyrenaica, whence Sicily, in 664, had been invaded. Crete had been captured and turned Muslim; the Byzantines, and the emperor Constans himself, had been beaten – to the Muslims' own surprise – in a naval battle off Marmaris in Lycia; and early raiding expeditions developing into regular sieges throughout the later seventh century had been reaching the walls of Constantinople itself. The legend goes that the warrior Abu Eyüp, whose mosque is now famous, fell in the attack of 669, and applauded the Janissaries, his Turkish successors, from his forgotten tomb as they broke through in 1453.

The little Phoenician towns of the Palestine and Syrian coasts had been left derelict by the wars of Heraclius, and were rebuilt – the walls of Akka (Acre), bonded with ancient columns, being sunk bodily on wooden platforms till they settled on the bottom of the sea. Meanwhile Greek, Coptic or Syrian workmen continued to build ships for their new masters, and a Byzantine raid on Egypt in 672 inspired the first Muslim arsenal (which is an Arabic word). Clysma, or Qulzum – the predecessor of Suez and only about a mile away from it – reinstated the canal which Trajan had dug and which was now called after the Lord of the Faithful, Amir al-Mu'minin; from here 3,000 camel-loads of corn a week would be exported through the Red Sea for Mecca, and merchants would come from the south of France to pick up the India and China trade. By the time of the Crusades, the whole transport was working in an organized and lucrative way, and we may close with a description of the Customs in Alexandria under Saladin, as given by Ibn Jubair, a Muslim pilgrim from Spain:

'The day of our landing, one of the first things we saw was the coming on board of the agents of the Sultan to record all that had been brought in the ship. All the Muslims in it were brought forward one by one, and their names and descriptions, together with the names of their countries, recorded. Each was questioned as to what merchandise or money he had, that he might pay *zakat*, without any enquiry as to what portion of it had been in their possession for a complete year and what had not. … Ahmed ibn Hassan of our number was called down to be questioned as to the news of the west and as to the ship's cargo. … The Muslims were then ordered to take their belongings, and what remained of their provisions, to the shore, where there were attendants responsible for them and for carrying to the Custom-house all that they had brought. There they were called one by one, and the possessions of each were produced. The Customs was packed to choking. All their goods, great and small, were searched and confusedly thrown together, while hands were thrust into their waistbands in search of what might be within. The owners were then put on oath whether they had aught else not discovered. During all this, because of the confusion of hands and the excessive throng, many possessions disappeared. After this scene of abasement and shame, for which we pray God to recompense us amply, they [the pilgrims] were allowed to go.' (*The Travels of Ibn Jubair*, trans. R.J.C. Brocklehurst, London 1952, p. 31.) This familiar and profitable scene, so far as the southern provinces were concerned, was now closed to the Byzantine Custom-house officials for ever.

The Coming of the Seljuks

Arab raiding and counter-raiding continued in a desultory way across the Taurus, producing a life comparable to that of the English-Scottish border, with the same sort of ballads blossoming out of similar conditions. These had become more or less stabilized, and were scarcely realized in Constantinople when, in the eleventh century, the second dangerous wound was given to her defences by the gradual infiltration and final downpour of the Seljuk Turks.

The nomads of Arabia had centuries of Greco-Roman intercourse behind them, and soon reinstated the trade routes. But the Turks in their first impact were enemies of cities, not so much from malice as from an exclusive interest in the grazing of their innumerable flocks: in his book on government, Nizam ul-Mulk reports a million sheep as being given to Alptigin in Transoxiana, and it was under their gradual nibbling progress that the cities disappeared.

Great civilizations went under in Central Asia – the Samanids in Bukhara to begin with, and the Ghaznevids with their provinces stretched out round Afghanistan. After their defeat, the gates of Persia lay open, and one landscape after another was left in ruins. Merv, chosen as capital in 1043, was destroyed by later waves of invasion, so that scarce a trace remains. In 1045 the first raid was made across the Armenian border, whose last independent centre was soon wiped out at Ani: its gaunt walls and churches are still standing, in a desolation as empty as a Scottish highland, along the Russian border. The Christian churches remained derelict round Van and Akthamar.

Soon Antioch, Edessa (Urfa) and Trebizond (Trabzon) were raided, Caesaraea (Kayseri) and Iconium (Konya) were stormed, and the Aegean shores were reached: the whole of eastern Anatolia became depopulated or dotted with the yurts of Central Asia. In this desolation, in a wide and flowing landscape punctuated with volcanoes, the battle of Manzikert was fought in 1071, and the emperor Romanos Diogenes defeated. The whole plateau lay at the mercy of the invaders.

If one had to be conquered by a Central Asian horde, the Seljuks were in the long run among the less disastrous. They had a remarkable gift for government, and their tents had moved round the trade routes of Samarkand and Bukhara for over two hundred years, during which interval they had become converted to Islam. A further vital respite was given to Anatolia by their pause and establishment in Persia, where the 'Great Seljuks' enrolled themselves as defenders of the Baghdad Caliph, who crowned them 'Sultans of East and West' (1058). When, soon after the battle of Manzikert, Malik Shah became their ruler, they were already a civilized community, delicately guided in the Persian art of government by great civil servants of the vanquished regimes like Nizam ul-Mulk, whose devoted labours were to cradle one conqueror after another into the well-established ways. I have often thought that the outstandingly civilizing influence of Persian bureaucracy in the eastern world has not been given as much credit as it deserves.

About 1077, six years or so after Manzikert, Malik Shah appointed Suleyman, a young Seljuk relative, to be governor of Rum or Anatolia. He had already proved himself an expert diplomat, and the civil wars of the Byzantines had helped him to enter Constantinople in a friendly way as an ally of the emperor Michael; other claimants or usurpers then asked his help, and he had three times accompanied one or the other as far as the coasts of Marmara with their long, wooded peninsulas and rich plains. The third time he decided not to turn his horse's head round again, but declared himself Sultan, and settled his capital at Nicaea (1078). Within eight years he had also declared himself independent of the Great Seljuks in Persia, and in 1134, forty-eight years later, under his grandson, Konya became the capital of Rum.

A very intricate and broken history fills this interval of time, a constant shifting of alliances and powers among Turk, Byzantine and the Crusaders, whose first wave reached Constantinople twenty-five years after Manzikert had brought its permanent alteration to eastern Mediterranean history. During the two centuries that followed, the Seljuks and the lesser dynasties that clustered round them had time to leave their noble and enduring signature on the lands they had conquered – an architecture unrivalled in its kind. They became enterprising traders and, under the strong and genuine influence of Islam, developers of what one may call a welfare state. Little remains, yet the splendour of their hospitals and schools can still be seen – spared by time and war and earthquake – in Mardin, Kayseri, Sivas, Amasya, Erzurum, or at Divrik among the scarcely known Euphrates gorges, or where Old Malatya suns itself round its beautiful crumbling mosque and grand infirmary.

The roads, with the comfort of those who travelled through bitter and fatiguing climates along them, were their particular care, and the Seljuk bridges are among the joys of Turkish travel in lonely places. I can conjure them up, still with a feeling of rapture, at some unexpected corner where the pack-animals have long disappeared and the motor has scarcely come. There were seven such bridges, my guide told me, in the valley of the Gök Su (the ancient Calycadnus), where now only one – massive, elegant and useful – remains under the singing of its pines. In the arid distances between them, the night's rest would be fixed by the windowless enclosure of the caravanserai, beautiful, functional and austere in its proportions, with a single gateway in the centre of the blank wall delicately carved. As one's animals stumbled past the guard-rooms, the court would spread its arcade round the small mosque in the centre, and the merchant would settle with his packs in a room built against the enclosing wall; with his small cooking fire in sight through the open door and his drivers asleep beside it, he could hear his rested animals munching their fodder through the night. One might still, if one wished, follow the ancient routes by these stages, finding gaps where many have crumbled away; but many are still beautiful if not intact in the vastness of their landscapes. I have often wished to make such a leisurely journey, from Ankara to Baghdad and the Holy Cities for instance, or along the Persian stretch of the Silk Road, from where Sarakhs lies (rarely visited and only in fine weather) on the Afghan border, across the Salt Desert where – looking from an aeroplane – I have seen a built-up, unused bit of sand-blown masonry probably left by Seljuk or later Mongol; and so under the lee of the Elburz range and across the Anatolian border towards Sivas or Kayseri or Konya, wherever the capital of the time happened to be. An old friend of mine in Baghdad was educated in Istanbul, and used to make two of these journeys every year on his way to and from school – forty days along the two rivers and across the plateau, in a carriage shaped like a tube under a circular awning where the traveller could lie and stretch himself between one jolt and another.

The records of this great trading nation are scattered more or less everywhere, but chiefly in the highlands which were the centre of their power. When they died out, at the beginning of the fourteenth century, after the Mongol invasion, subsidiary dynasties of the Turkish family continued to flourish, nearly all of them for another century, and some, like the Menteshe of Aydin, till well into the fifteenth. The Karamanli lasted till about 1483, and held the southern passes to beyond Konya, and rode twice yearly through those pleasant hills, whose cedar forests Antony had once given to Cleopatra for her navies. Their summer and winter capitals were Konya and Alanya, which the Seljuks had captured in 1220 and soon made the richest harbour of the coast.

Here, as in the walls of Diyarbakir or Bayburt, the Seljuk art of fortification is seen in all its excellence, crowning – with well-cut stone and finely wrought inscriptions – the conquered Byzantine walls. There is even a remnant of the earlier Greek in Alanya's wall, with a low gate used when Coracesium was the pirates' hold and Pompey in the offing; it became Candalore under the Byzantines, until the Seljuk sultan Alaeddin made it his winter capital and called it by his name, and built its slipway and covered dock, which stands as intact as when it was new at the water's edge beside a splendid tower.

The whole of this coast, which we have already travelled along through the classic age, should be revisited for these later centuries, when Seljuk and Armenian, Byzantine and Crusader shuffled each other in and out of a kaleidoscope of temporary fiefs and fortified places. A Turkish bridge across the Calycadnus, where Frederick Barbarossa was drowned, leads under the rounded bastions of Silifke – ceded to the knights of St John – through lands that the Lesser Armenians had seized and fortified. Corycos and Anamur, the most romantic medieval castles, still capture one with their enchantment on the shore.

The Seljuks raided, inhabited, fortified and prosperously exploited these magic beaches: but their power lay in the uplands that had once nourished the Hittite armies, and had fought Alexander, and had saved Byzantium under the Isaurian dynasty – and were now taken from Byzantium for ever. This was the second hammer-stroke of fate which, after the loss of her southern provinces, prepared her slow catastrophe. After Manzikert, the Byzantine rulers could rely on mercenaries only.

The Third Catastrophe, of the Crusades

'Seen in the perspective of history', one is interested to hear Sir Steven Runciman say, 'the whole Crusading movement was a vast fiasco.' However romantically one may feel towards it, this sober conclusion is not to be denied. When the Fourth Crusade had done its worst, Villehardouin's chronicle shows the nordic chivalry trying to make a western empire work in the Byzantine ruin, and the picture has a nightmare quality, as if dinosaurs, long extinct, lost, doomed and destructive, were suddenly moving through a settled countryside. 'In the long sequence of interaction and fusion between Orient and Occident out of which our civilization has grown', Runciman sums up, 'the Crusades were a tragic and destructive episode.' 'So much courage, and so little honour, so much devotion and so little understanding.'

The damage done not only weakened the Byzantine state for the coming shock of the Ottomans; it also, through the two centuries of this spectacular adventure, so embittered the Christian-Muslim relation as to destroy any possibility of gradual toleration, of a way of life unified enough to throw its influence into the love-hate system which is a part of the orientals' philosophy, so that one is sometimes inclined to think that they enjoy it.

Not only their border sagas, but a number of historical incidents show this feeling. No less than six Seljuk sultans, ousted or deposed, found refuge and kindness in Constantinople, and remembered and were grateful; and when the Latins stormed it, the exiled emperor was received in Konya. In the first crusading year, when the Byzantines were able to use the knights for the recapture of Nicaea, the Sultan's surrendered family was restored to him without ransom by the Emperor; and even a century and more later, in a war between Byzantine and Seljuk, when the emperor Theodore Lascaris was thrown from his horse, the sultan Keyhüsrev helped him to remount and to depart. The Sultan was killed in this battle, and Lascaris wept when the body was brought him, and gave it honourable burial by the Muslim rite. There was a mosque for the visiting Muslims in Constantinople, which the French in the Fourth Crusade burned down.

Boorish and intolerant, except towards its own narrow code, the First Crusade had already shown symptoms of difficulties ahead when it reached Constantinople in 1096. The emperor Alexius shepherded it skilfully, first to the retaking of Nicaea and then across the dust-blown summer plains of Konya, round the worst of the Taurus, by Germaniceia (Marash), to where the marshes of Orontes flow to the ramparts of Antioch. In 1098 these were taken; and just over a year later Jerusalem fell. The glory and profit of this achievement on the one hand, and the loss and capture of Edessa (Urfa) and her Crusader king on the other, inspired the Second Crusade, in 1147, with a wave of enthusiasm which failed to survive the rigours of the march across the Taurus. In 1187, the Third Crusade, or rather that contingent that had taken the land route, disintegrated as far as Anatolia was concerned, after the drowning of its leader Barbarossa under the walls of Silifke. The Crusaders had passed the bleached bones of the Byzantine dead on the plateau on their way, and no later Christian army came from the north across the Seljuk lands. For the Fourth Crusade, the armies gathered in 1202 in Venice, got into debt to the Venetians for their transport, were granted a postponement on condition of helping in the assault on the Christian city of Zara, and finally sailed for Constantinople with an exiled and worthless nephew of the Emperor, a claimant who would free them of their debts if once seated on the throne.

If one is defenceless, it is safest to be poor; and Constantinople, though passing through one of its too frequent domestic crises, was yet the richest city in the world. In 1071, the very year of Manzikert, the Norman adventurers on their way south had captured Bari on the Adriatic and shown that an eastern direction was already in their mind. When the First Crusade had taken Antioch, the trouble with them began.

During the Second Crusade, Louis VII of France had been advised, but refused, to attack Constantinople; during the Third, Barbarossa had been tempted, but passed on. No such scruples troubled the old and blind Venetian doge, Dandolo. The plan was in his mind before ever the fleet left Venice, while a treaty of commercial peace was actually being negotiated with Egypt – the ostensible target of the crusade. The Pope, shocked by the attack on Zara, excommunicated the Venetians, without disturbing the peace of mind of the Doge.

In Constantinople, the usurper was enthroned, and a winter followed of fiercely rising anger on both sides. Hunger and poverty were making themselves felt, and the sight of the strangers strolling armed about their city maddened the populace beyond endurance. The young emperor was torn from his seat and killed and another elected, and the Crusaders decided to make the city their own. The Great Palace was stormed, and for three days the soldiers were given leave to sack and destroy and ravish the treasures of the ancient world.

This was the third and greatest blow that befell the great empire established by Constantine nine centuries before. The mainstay of the civilization of eastern Europe went with it, and though the ruin was not yet complete, the breach was never repaired. History forgives crimes, but not blindness, and the final act, 250 years later, was now prepared.

The Naval Nemesis

While the Crusaders were breaking into the city, the Byzantine nobles offered the crown to Theodore Lascaris. But he refused it, for there was nothing to be done. He made one desperate vain appeal to the Varangian guard to carry on the fight, and then slipped across the Bosphorus, with many other citizens, to the Asiatic shore.

Theodore built up his new kingdom round Nicaea, in the country that stretches from the Aegean to the Black Sea, from Mysian Olympus (the Olympus of the *Iliad*) south and east almost to Ankara on the Seljuk border. This is comfortable country, that dips into fertile irrigated valleys full of a feeling of safety and seclusion, a country not too rough for the farmers and yet where an enemy could be ambushed if he came. Here Theodore and his son-in-law Vatatzes, and grandson Theodore II, were crowned and all the regular formalities complied with; and from here, when they had nursed their empire back to strength and power, the re-entry into Constantinople was made. A Nicaean commander, reconnoitering near the great walls early on 25 July 1261, found the city practically empty and entered it at dawn. The Lascaris, in the person of Theodore II's young son, came to an obscure and violent end, and Michael VIII Palaeologus, ex-regent and a member of the aristocratic party, opened two centuries of his dynasty's rule, the last in Byzantium.

At the time of the Greek re-entry, the Latin kingdom had spluttered out almost of its own accord – a misfit in history. The kingdom of Nicaea, under the admirable management of Vatatzes and the intellectual leadership of his son, had grown in prosperity and importance, and held its station as head of the Byzantine empire above all the attacks and intrigues of family rivalry in Epirus or Trebizond, or among Serbs and Bulgars in the north, or aspirants in Europe. Its territory gradually enlarged itself to halt the Trebizond cousins' westerly expansion and to hem the diminished Latins into the north Marmara shore. The attacks of the Seljuks, which would certainly have been made, were providentially interfered with by the Mongol invasions, and Vatatzes was able to build his frontier fortresses and settle his borderland with soldiers in the traditional Byzantine way.

All this was adequate for Nicaea, but not for Constantinople and its international importance as the gateway of the straits. The city when recovered was squalid with ruin, and the means of recovery had gone. The void of its armies had to be filled with mercenaries, Seljuk or others, who went over to the other side when their pay became irregular. This, as we have seen, was the blow that Manzikert and the Seljuk invasions had dealt. The Latins had exposed and exasperated it; and soon the fourth and perhaps the most deadly wound, imperceptibly given and increasingly operative, became obvious to all, for the Byzantines had gradually lost their supremacy at sea.

In early days, the Arab sea-faring threat had been met with the secret weapon of 'Greek fire', through which the Byzantines were able to hold the sea in spite of the loss of Palestinian, Syrian and Egyptian shipyards. But by the twelfth century, at the siege of Acre during the Third Crusade, Saladin had got hold of and was using this weapon, and by that time the Seljuks in Alanya were sedulously developing their navy. Commercial transport had long been increasing among the southern Europeans, particularly the Italian maritime republics, and the Crusades brought a great deal of direct traffic between European and Arab ports, cutting out the Byzantines altogether: a sort of organization comparable to modern tourism enlarged the ships for pilgrims (and also for the Crusaders' horses) and established the seasonal dates of their sailings.

In May 1082, eleven years after Manzikert, the emperor Alexius Comnenus, surrounded by enemies and with the Norman threat in the Adriatic developing, made the first disastrous treaty with Venice: it allowed unrestricted trade free of all customs' dues throughout the empire, and conceded several warehouses in Constantinople itself and three quays opposite Galata on the Golden Horn. It was the Adriatic queen's foundation stone.

Nearly two hundred years later, in March 1261, Michael Palaeologus tried to neutralize the Venetians by signing a similar treaty with their Genoese rivals, including a military alliance, the same freedom from customs, and commercial quarters in the chief ports. Within the next decade he improved on what it is only fair to call a necessity rather than a policy, by making new treaties with both powers at the expense of further concessions, so that he could play off one against the other in the gathering discords of Europe. By this time the Byzantine merchants had been practically swept off their own seas and there could be no financial recovery in sight.

So shackled and so doomed, with the Ottomans appearing, we turn from Constantinople that had been Byzantium and was about to become Istanbul.

86, 87   The Black Sea has a strangely different magic from the Aegean: the spell is that of a witch rather than an enchantress, and one cannot sail along it without noticing, both in feeling and in weather, the vague, indefinite influences of the northern steppes and the Slavonic atmosphere like a cloud on the horizon. Pretty fishing villages, Byzantine castles, small, well-built towns with their roadsteads now turning into harbours, the blackish half-moon beaches that have given the sea its name, and the variegated forested slopes above them, nearly always topped with cloud – they build a landscape nearer to Europe than to Asia, but different from either. A pleasant tour from one to the other of these little centres is arranged by the Turkish Maritime Services once a fortnight in summer.

88   The monastery of Sumela was built and dedicated to the Virgin in AD 472, in a thickly wooded valley some 30 miles from Trebizond (Trabzon). Clinging to the naked wall of the precipice, its only access is by an outer stairway that opens on a narrow space jutting from the sheer rock and just wide enough to hold the buildings. These run to four storeys, added during the nineteenth century, and are not interesting; but the church, encased in a shallow rock overhang, has four layers of frescoes, much knocked about and wantonly destroyed, but still keeping their background of Byzantine colour and splendour. (See p. 170 for the saving of an angel's head.)

89, 90   Trapezus, modern Trebizond or Trabzon, was founded by colonists from Miletus in the eighth century BC. It became part of the lands of Pontus, and so figured in the epic wars of Mithridates; it was later conquered by Rome, and flourished under Hadrian and Justinian. But its great age followed the sack of Constantinople in 1204 by the Crusaders, when the Grand

Comneni, David and Alexius, captured it with the help of Queen Thamar of Georgia, and spread their power westward, to Sinope and Heraklea along the Black Sea coast. Their advance was stopped, first by the rival Byzantines of Nicaea, and secondly by the Seljuks with the capture of Sinope. Trebizond became a vassal to the Sultan of Iconium; but its empire, fed by the trade for the Bosphorus that could here avoid Seljuk customs, nevertheless continued to flourish, until it too fell to the Ottoman Turks a few years after the fall of Constantinople.

One can still drive down the road by which Xenophon is said to have come with his Ten Thousand, and the cathedral of St Sophia, shown here, is now a museum and intact with all its carving. Many of the best frescoes have been destroyed, but what was left was restored in the 1950s by the Russell Trust.

91, 92, 93, 94   Antioch (Antakya) was founded by Alexander's general, Seleucus I Nicator, who became King of Babylonia and Syria when the great conqueror's lands were divided. The site was carefully chosen, both for defence, where its walls climb the steep and rocky hill, and for trade, where the wealth of Asia could find its way from Persia across the Euphrates or up through Mesopotamia from Hormuz in the Persian Gulf. Capital of the Seleucid Kingdom, it became the capital of Syria under Rome, and kept its wealth, its skill in arts and learning, and its decadent magnificence through wars and earthquakes and religious schisms until the coming of the Arabs. The first Christian church, where Peter is said to have preached, is still shown cut in the rock behind it. The First Crusade was held up here besieging the city, until Tancred climbed one of its towers in the night. It is now a quietly prosperous country town with the Orontes running through it, the only vestiges of its splendour being in the civic museum, which contains the largest and most important collection of Roman mosaics – of the second century AD – in all Turkey.

Plate 91, from the House of the Drunken Dionysus, shows the inebriated god leaning on a young satyr, while the wine spilling from his cup is lapped up by a panther. The Bacchic dancers in plate 92 come from the House of Dionysus and Ariadne. In the first panel, the satyr holds a syrinx (pipe), the maenad a pair of cymbals. In the second, the maenad shakes a tambourine in one hand, and holds a thyrsus in the other. The satyr, an older man or silenus, holds a cap. The life-like birds in plate 93 are from the House of the Red Pavement. Plate 94 shows a Negro fisherman (so-called from his hat, which is characteristic of fishermen) from the House of the Calendar. He carries rods in his right hand, and with the left supports a pole with baskets at each end.

95, 96, 97, 98 Akthamar: a small island opposite Gevas on the southern coast of Lake Van, now – only recently – open to visitors. A church built in AD 915 by Gagik Ardzruni, king of what was then Vaspurakan Armenia, is one of the best preserved of the Armenian churches and most remarkable for its rich exterior decoration, perhaps inspired by the Byzantine. It includes figures of Christ and the saints in flat relief, fantastic animals, and a fascinating frieze of men, animals and birds in a meandering vine. The church took six years to build. The monastery beside it is a ruin, and the island itself is rarely visited because of the scarcity of boats on Lake Van.

99–100, 101, 102, 103–4 Göreme and Bin-bir Kilise (the Thousand-and-one Churches) are about 190 miles from Ankara and 60 from Kayseri, in the most fantastic strip of landscape in Cappadocia. In a wide valley open to the sun, the red and yellow earth has been modelled by winds and weathers into hard little pointed cones which the monks of the seventh century excavated into chapels and cells and churches. The strange formation is said to be a layer of ashes from Ercyas, the neighbouring volcano which, as we have seen, had already been responsible for the prehistoric civilization of Çatal Hüyük. The neat, whitewashed houses of Ürgüb and other villages grew up among this strange outcrop, which incidentally grows the best wine in Turkey (a wine press is found in one of the excavated monasteries, also cut in the stone). Inside the chapels and churches many paintings are found, with colours still bright and particularly vivid in their perpetual twilight.

105 The weaving of carpets is one of the most ancient crafts in Anatolia. It used to supply the palaces of the ancient Persian kings, particularly through the centre of the plateau between Gördes and Malatya, where the best carpets come from, and where almost every household owns one of the old-fashioned upright looms.

106 Bread is baked in the old way familiar to all the Middle East in country places, where every household makes it for itself. The paste of flour and water is stretched by being tossed from arm to arm, and – when as fine as a thin circular piece of cardboard – is thrown to cook for a few minutes on a sheet of metal laid upon the fire. In a larger community, there may be an oven of hard-baked earth, and here the bread will be tossed from a cushion against the inner side of the oven roof, and skilfully picked off when crisp, before it falls.

107 Göreme. The interior of one of the rock-cut churches showing the abstract, rather crude, designs which characterize the Iconoclast periods of Byzantine art (eighth and ninth centuries), when representations of Christ and the saints were forbidden.

108 Göreme. After the defeat of Iconoclasm, the painting of traditional religious scenes was resumed. Those in this church include Christ the Judge (in the dome), angels, saints, and at the back the Crucifixion.

109 The dome of St Sophia, Istanbul, is one of the greatest architectural triumphs in the world. It was built under Justinian to replace the older church, which had been destroyed in the Nika riots of AD 532.

It remains perhaps the greatest of church interiors – first built by two Ionian Greeks, Anthemius and Isidore, of Tralles (Aydin) and Miletus respectively. Its dome was rebuilt in AD 989 by Tiridates, the Armenian architect of Ani, when earthquakes had twice shattered the earlier ones. The boldness of their conception lay in the high-buttressed east and west ends, crowned with half-domes supporting the stress of the centre. The rich decoration has largely vanished, but the mosaic portraits of the emperors have recently been cleared of the whitewash that covered them. The names of the early caliphs hanging in large targes of black and white remind us that on the very day of the conquest the qibla (a spear, later formalized as the mihrab niche) was turned to Mecca and the call to prayer was heard.

110 The base of the obelisk of Theodosius the Great in the ancient Hippodrome of Istanbul. Placed there in about AD 390, it shows the Emperor with the victor's wreath in his hand and his family and suite around him. The erection of the obelisk – 65 feet high – is shown on the northern face of the base. When the work was nearly in place, the engines that held the cords could raise it only to a fraction of an inch below the required

height: the great work seemed to be collapsing when the engineer thought of wetting the cords; they tightened in drying, and in this way lifted the huge mass into place.

111–12　The long southern beaches, between one small harbour and another, are protected from the north wind by the wall of Mount Taurus behind them.

113　Alanya, the ancient Coracesium, headquarters of the pirates whom Pompey defeated and pacified: a record of its Greek origin can still be seen in one small gateway in the wall. The beauty of its situation, leaning against the southern slope of Taurus, gave it the name of Calonoros (the beautiful place) or Candelor in the Middle Ages, when Byzantium left a church in its high citadel, and the Seljuks took it. When Ibn Batuta travelled there, in 1333, he found the Karamanli sultans in possession; Sultan Alaeddin gave it his name and adopted it as his winter capital, moving across the limestone ridges to Karaman in summer. The Seljuks and Karamanlis have left Alanya with the best monuments that remain there: the fine walls, the tower built in 1226, unique of its kind, and the dock with its five arches, where the swift, light boats called 'swallows' could dart out to sea.

92

91

93 94

105

In 1952, when I travelled about in western Anatolia, the traces of the Greek war then thirty years old were much more apparent than they are today. A feeling of havoc still hung over the coast, where paved quays stood abandoned, and new inhabitants, unfamiliar to their surroundings, gathered in long Turkish silences round a few café tables inland, well away from the disturbing litany of the sea. Muslims from Bulgaria or Macedonia, roughly dumped at short notice on the harassed Ankara government, were already established, with tobacco in their fields and geese in their ditches, in villages whose Greeks had been transplanted to Salonica. There was a hotel in Izmir – of the sort described by the *Guide bleu* as *précaire* – and up and down the length of the Maeander valley there were rumoured to be two bedrooms with basins and running water, one at Nazilli and one at Denizli, as I well remember. Travelling was old-fashioned and uncertain, but it had its compensations, and a porter would offer one a chair to sit on while waiting for one's train. Trains are never too slow for me, and Turkey was all that one could wish for in this respect: nowhere else had I seen the smoke blown ahead of its engine while the thing was in motion; the long, several-day journeys through the vast, laborious land, with their casual acquaintance from compartment to compartment, and conductors' visits between stations, explaining to docile countrymen the unreasonable difference between first and second class; the kind offers of food (no one need ever travel hungry in Turkey), and the immediate generous hospitality – all these things I remember, connected with the Turkish trains.

The 1922 war must have wiped away many Byzantine traces, for apart from Istanbul one came upon little in the countryside to remind one of the great episode of 1124 years. The chapels were mostly wrecked, if one could find them at all; the sites now excavated, like Myra (Demre) or Alahan, had not yet been touched; and even Ürgüp and Bin-bir Kilise (the Thousand-and-one Churches), which had been excavated and painted in the gnome-like hummocks of tufa before the Seljuks came – even they demanded an expedition and the spending of a night in the care-taker's garden. Nisibis (Nusaybin) on the Syrian frontier, with its very early church and St Sergius's tomb, and air of Mesopotamian antiquity about its pilasters, was a long way from anywhere, and its hotel could daunt the bravest; and the nearby Byzantine ruins and cisterns of Dara, with the bedouin women in crimson and magenta velvet, drawing water from the open desert wells; and the monastery school of Deir Zafiran tucked in its hills with rich Justinian carving still intact – these, and no doubt many more that I never succeeded in reaching, were so chancy in the matter of roads, transport and permits that the very thought of them demanded a good span of leisure. The little churches of Tur Abdin in their moonlike landscape have hardly been visited, I think, since Gertrude Bell travelled and wrote about them, and even the Islamic monuments – the school and arcades of Mardin and the mosque of Dunaisir on the ancient road from Syria to Euphrates – even these at that time could turn spiky at any moment with police.

The memory of trouble was too fresh in south-east Turkey and right up to the neighbourhood of Van, and it was along the northern, Black Sea coast, to Trebizond (Trabzon) and westward, that an older and more peaceful atmosphere persisted, between little towns, or whitewashed houses dotted singly along the high, dark, wooded slopes. It is remarkable how much security is expressed by a building in a landscape that feels it safe to stand alone. Fragments of walls, the neatly built castles of the Comneni, stood on headlands or in the curve of bays among enclosures of tea or tobacco which the moist climate now produces. The churches of Trebizond itself were dilapidated or turned to store-rooms, except for the cathedral of St Sophia, which was being restored by the Russell Trust; but the city walls still climbed the ridge to one high palace-window, and many of the monasteries in the hills around, though turned to other purposes, are preserved intact. Only Sumela – remote among forests in its valley – lies deserted with the saints of her frescoes strewn upon the ground. We found an angel's head lying unharmed, and gathered it to take to Trebizond museum; and as we drove back I heard the driver say to his assistant: 'These people are carting that *antika* away'; so instead of waiting till next morning when the rumour and its trouble would have spread, we knocked on the Director's door till he came and took the trophy from us, much surprised.

Trebizond was able to catch the trade from Persia and the East on its way to the Bosphorus. It therefore flourished after the Crusaders had sacked Constantinople, and continued to do so until the Ottomans – or Osmanlis, as the dynasty is more correctly called – moved eastward, in 1461, eight years after Byzantium's final fall.

The whole progress of their advance was gradual though steady, as historic time is counted – an infiltration rather than a wave, very different from the first impact of Seljuk or Mongol devastations. The legend goes that Ertugrul, with 440 Turkish horsemen of his tribe, came riding west from Khorasan across the Euphrates towards the end of the thirteenth century, when barely a generation had gone by after the expulsion of the Latins from Constantinople. A border skirmish was going on in no-man's-land, and the Turkish stranger, asking no questions, cantered in to help the weaker side. Having tilted the odds in their favour, he discovered that it was the Seljuk Alaeddin whom he had rescued. He became his vassal, and settled near the Byzantine frontier in the north, and adopted the Seljuk crescent on his banners. His son Othman beat the Greeks at Nicomedia, and heard on his deathbed of the conquest of Bursa (Brusa); the two brothers, his grandsons Orhan and Alaeddin, made this their capital, based on a strong quadrilateral with Pergamon, Nicomedia and Nicaea – all conquered before the middle of the fourteenth century. They were superlatively placed for attack, out of the main stream of Mongol invasion, and with no enemy in the south except the Karamanians.

The Anatolian world was being shaken by Mongol and Mameluke wars, but was too long settled, and was too Muslim on the whole, to be tempting to Turkish nomads descending, hungry for land. Before the end of the century, the Armenians of Cilicia (1375), the Seljuks of Syria, and Acre, the last stronghold on the diminished coast of the Crusaders (1291), had all melted away before the Egyptian armies: the hordes of restless warriors anxious for a holy war (*jihad*) and its rewards found in the little Osmanli frontier state an open door. The young sultans had no military problem such as had maimed the Byzantines; they had all the soldiers they needed, of their own race and with their own beliefs, and were able to draw on loot from the enemy for pay.

The Seljuks had lingered in Persia before reaching Anatolia, and drew their administrators in large measure from that highly civilized store-room. When they arrived, with the Baghdad Caliph's blessing, they were already members of the great and fairly uniform Islamic-Arabic world; the Osmanlis were Muslims too, but of the Gazi or frontier-fighting variety – passionately Sunni in the orthodox tradition, with swords rather than Qurans in their minds. What they needed was a method for aggression, and the system of attack which Ertugrul brought with him continued to be used for centuries, winning battle after battle – the irregulars being expended against men or guns or walls, till the main attack of the infantry breaking through them could carry its full weight.

Orhan, and even more so his brother Alaeddin, built up the standing army on foundations that also went on from generation to generation until they became superannuated in the Turkish decline. They were far ahead of anything in Europe when they began, and many comparisons are made between the licence and disorder of the westerners and the regular pay and strict and quiet discipline of the Turks. The cavalry (Sipahis) were rewarded with land, which was supposed not to be sold or handed on to their children, and for which they were bound to give military service. They were 2,400 to begin with, and 4,000 under Suleyman the Great, and formed the Sultan's bodyguard, one half of them camping on each side of his tent.

The infantry (Piyade), when it had become too highly paid and privileged to be safe, was given the counterweight of a corps of Janissaries, also invented at this time. They were chosen and trained from among the captive Christian children or – if these were insufficient – drawn as a tax from the conquered lands. Well treated, carefully educated, and forcibly converted, they were free to rise in the army and later in civilian service also, to such wealth and power that Muslims, too, eventually and unobtrusively managed to be allowed into the corps. Their antique uniform can still be seen, worn by the band that plays inside the walls of Rumeli Hisar on the summer Bosphorus on Sundays, with the strip of white wool hanging to the shoulder that commemorates the blessing of a dervish as he drew his sleeve across one little cadet's head when first the corps was formed.

The Janissaries were slaves, under the (nominally) absolute authority of the Sultan, whose household they formed. 'What is your will, my servants?' the young Murat IV asked them, when he met them in their revolt. Apart from this status there was no tradition of class among them, nor any rank to which they might not be promoted – unlike the cavalry with their estates and long Muslim tradition, who could easily develop into *derebeys* or landed gentry, which in the long run they did as soon as the rule against inheriting was relaxed. The natural social prejudice in the new government therefore came to divide, not – as one might have expected – the conquerors and the conquered (out of whose ranks the Janissaries had sprung), so much as these aristocrats and democrats of the army, whose rivalry, if it was to be rendered harmless, needed a strong hand able to hold the reins of both parties. It made absolute rule essential.

This formidable engine of aggression was hammered out by the two grandsons of Ertugrul where Bursa hangs on its hillside as if it were a part of the mists and vineyards. The forests that festoon it pour the waters of the Mysian Olympus to irrigate the plain. It still appears as one of the most unified of Turkish towns, though the recent damage to its oldest mosque and the accidental burning of the bazaar have altered it a good deal. The early rulers lie under their turbans on the citadel, or in the mausoleums of the Muradiye, under peaceful plane trees, and the Ottoman story moves on from them with the fourth generation, across the Sea of Marmara to Thrace.

Edirne (Adrianople) became the second capital, and is still today – in spite of disasters as recent as this century – a pleasantly livable place, in a green oasis on the fertile, but uninteresting, Thracian plain. According to Busbecq, Ferdinand of Austria's ambassador at the Turkish court, Suleyman the Great was in the habit of spending his winters there, and 'not returning to Constantinople until the frogs begin to be a nuisance with their croaking', which no doubt goes on today in the marshy land (*Letters*, trans. E. S. Forster, Oxford 1927). In this city, perhaps better than anywhere, one finds the dignity and solidity of the earliest Osmanli building, developing with the passing of two centuries into the Selimiye mosque of Sinan, one of the loveliest and most graceful in the world.

The city was captured by Murat I in 1361, and here – having temporarily defeated the Karamanians in the south – he chose red for the background of the Turkish crescent banner, and carried it northward to open the long series of the Balkan wars. Serbia, Bosnia, Albania, with Hungarian and Polish allies, were defeated at Kossovo in 1389; before the victory was decided, a Serbian nobleman reached and stabbed the Sultan, who had time to give one decisive order to his reserve before he died. His son Beyazit succeeded him with no interruption, and the younger brother (who had fought at his side all day) was seized and killed in the tent where their father lay dead. This was the first of what one may call the ritual murders, which soon became law, of younger brothers who might cause trouble to the throne.

Another victory over Karamania, and then the last crusade making for Anatolia was annihilated at Nicopolis in 1396. All danger on the land frontiers was over; the west lay open, Greece was conquered, the invasion of Italy planned; and a respite for Constantinople was given only by a rival cataract of destruction descending with Tamerlane from Central Asia. At the battle of Ankara, Beyazit himself was captured (1402); the towns of Anatolia were wasted; and soon both conqueror and conquered died, and Beyazit's son brought his dead father back to Bursa, to the family tombs.

Mehmet I, in the sixth generation, after a time of trouble and another war with Karamania, enjoyed a short but honourable and moderate reign. He blinded but did not kill his brother, provided for him kindly, and would invite him to the palace when he came to Bursa – letting bygones be bygones in a way that still persists in the East, and has often surprised me (in Iraq in 1941, for instance), as if in such events the rigour of life rather than any human agency were blamed. When Mehmet came to die, at forty-seven, he sent two infant sons to the Byzantine emperor for safety, and was buried beside his own mosque in Bursa, in the most beautiful mausoleum of his time.

When the storm is coming, it is not a matter of great moment where the first drop falls. Ever since the defeat of the Crusade of Nicopolis, if not before, Constantinople had seen its fate approaching. But the Greek emperor gave an opening by sustaining a pretender, and Murat II drew a besieging army to face the walls. The troubles of Asia calling him away, or (according to one's belief) the miraculous apparition of the Virgin, saved the situation, and peace and tribute and a cession of cities were arranged in 1424. Twenty-nine years were still granted to the Byzantines, years that were full of weariness for the Osmanli sultan and brought him to his end. Unlike most of his line, he was warmhearted in his family affections, and his eldest and beloved son was dead. He had abdicated in favour of Mehmet, his second son, but the Hungarian war forced him back to the throne, to win the victory of Varna (1444). Again he retired; again the young Mehmet proved too inexperienced to hold the difficult place of power, and his father took the reins till he died in 1451. He was buried 'in a chapel without any roof, his grave nothing differing from that of the common Turks, which they say he commanded to be done in his last will, that the mercy and blessing of God might come to him by the shining of the sun and moon, and the falling of the rain and dew of heaven upon his grave' (Knolles, in 1610).

Mehmet the Conqueror was twenty-one when this happened, and for the third time he stepped into power. The most eloquent comment upon him is still the enigmatic, disquieting portrait by Gentile Bellini, and there is no other record of what adolescent bitterness crystallized into that refinement of civilized cruelty during the seven quiet years at Magnesia after his double failure in the world. He was not going to fail again. While his step-mother was welcoming him on his succession, her infant son was being murdered in his bath.

During 1452 the last siege of Constantinople was prepared by both sides, and at dawn on 29 May 1453 Mehmet's last assault opened against the gate of St Romanus, where the walls begin to dip towards the valley. Many accounts of this turning-point of history have been given, and Sir Steven Runciman's book, *The Fall of Constantinople*, should be read: no summary can begin to tell the story. When the more expendable waves had blunted the resistance, the Janissaries broke through the breaches; their cemetery with its white columns is still there, in a corner of the walls. About noon the Sultan rode with his suite to St Sophia, and commanded the muezzin's call to prayer. Constantinople was Istanbul.

Osmanli history continues under the impetus of remarkable sultans with a widening of scope but no basic change of direction. The conquered population were much more numerous than their victors, and both were soon collected from all sides to repopulate the desolate city. The conquered, or *rayas*, were organized with tolerance and liberality, free to practise and manage their religion under their own patriarch – which had always been a stumbling block in their relations with the west. 'There is no village, town, or city of any size in which there are not some Janissaries to guard the Christians, Jews, and other helpless folk from the attacks of malefactors', Busbecq writes when the great Suleyman was in power (Letter I). As the Osmanli tide of victory continued, the numbers of the Muslim converts increased, and when the Turkish power was at its height, 'out of ten Grand Viziers of this epoch, eight were renegades. ... At least twelve of her best generals and four of the most renowned admirals were supplied by ... Croatia, Albania, Bosnia, Greece, Hungary, Calabria and Russia, Christians and slaves.' (E. S. Creasy, *History of the Ottoman Turks*, London 1877, 2nd ed., p. 181.) From its very beginning – perhaps its best point –

the Turkish administration allowed a large amount of local self-government, in religious, municipal, and village life.

Mehmet's plans soared on from Istanbul. They failed before Belgrade and Rhodes, but Trebizond was captured, and Kaffa in the Crimea, and 1,500 young Genoese nobles were there entered among the Janissaries. Dreams of Italian subjection were encouraged by a landing at Otranto; and when the Sultan died – aged fifty-one – his army was already on the east shore of the Bosphorus for any destination his successor might choose.

The Osmanlis by this time were no longer the barbarians of the steppe. They had spent two centuries in the ruthless but sophisticated climate of the Levant, and even Selim the Grim, the most ruthless of them all, who nearly doubled the extent of the empire in his eight years' reign and wished to eliminate Christians and Shi'as altogether, wept over the elegy that was left him by the brother he murdered, and was himself known for the elegance of his verse. The drinking of wine had spread into the Muslim fold, and the Janissaries opened the taverns by force when they were closed; on the other hand, the strictness of education for the *ulema* (the official expounders of Muslim orthodoxy) was zealously watched over and encouraged. In the life of everyday, many of the habits of Byzantium continued, in spite of the barrier which religion built and has preserved to this day.

In spite of all this, the Osmanli state was still a Central Asian camp at heart; and the name of the 'Sublime Porte', the High Gate of the Royal Tent, was an accurate enough use of a familiar idea to describe the seat of government in its new surroundings. As in Rome during its early ventures, conquests were continually needed to expand and feed new conquests with their rewards: Selim I marched into the Persian capital and added Diyarbakir and Kurdistan to the eastern marches, and Egypt (with the massacre of the Mamelukes and of 50,000 inhabitants in Cairo) to the western. He was, later, said to have carried back the legacy of the Caliph's title from the last of the Abbasids, and the standard, sword and mantle of the Prophet, to Istanbul.

When he died, the climax of power came into the hands of Suleyman (1520–66), his son, who at twenty-six had already been viceroy during the Persian war and governor of Adrianople, and added ability, experience and a full treasury to the presence full of dignity and honour with which he impressed all those who met him.

Belgrade was captured in 1521, and Rhodes little over a year later; the 'Destruction of Mohacs' and practical elimination of the Hungarian army followed in 1526. In 1529, Suleyman reached the walls of Vienna, but was forced by weather and the unruly Janissaries and the heroism of the defence to leave it on 14 October – a date to be remembered in eastern Europe. In 1547, a five-year truce gave 30,000 ducats to his treasury as well as most of Hungary and Transylvania.

These epics can only be glanced at here, and spent themselves in regions far from the Turkey of today. The Mediterranean too was dominated, from Barbarossa's Mitylene to the Algerian coasts, by the buccaneering captains of that age – Greek, Arab, Croatian, Christian or slave. There is a description of the Spanish standard trailing in the Sea of Marmara behind the ship that came to bring the news of Djerbe – and of the admiral himself (Piale Pasha, a Croatian) leading the captive ships under Seraglio Point, where the Sultan sat. 'I myself', Busbecq writes and Knolles translates, 'saw him with the same countenance that he had always; with the same severity and gravity; as if the victory had nothing concerned him, nor anything chanced strange and unexpected; so capable was the great heart of that old sire of any fortune, were it never so great.' (Quoted in Creasy, p. 181.)

From beginning to end, the Ottoman dynasty had need of this severity to hold its power, and what private sorrows it cost them can never be known. Selim the Grim wept as he prayed after the victory in the mosque in Cairo, and Suleyman, who was a just man and merciful, sacrificed two sons and his friend and vizier, and many lesser victims. Nor did such actions appear to impair the loyalty of those who remained. The greatest number of brothers were strangled – nineteen altogether – in 1595 at the accession of Mehmet III, as is described in a document sent to Sir Edward Barton, English agent in Istanbul and later ambassador to the Porte:

'They were the male children then living of his father, by several wives, ... brought to kiss his hand, so that he should see them alive, the eldest of them was eleven. Their king brother told them not to fear, as he did not wish to do them any harm; but only to have them circumcised, according to the custom. And this was a thing that none of his ancestors had ever done, and directly they had kissed his hand they were circumcised, taken aside and dexterously strangled with handkerchiefs. This certainly seems a terrible and cruel thing, but it is the custom and people are used to it. On Saturday these innocent princes were washed and got ready according to custom, one after another according to age, and were laid in cypress coffins, and placed in the piazza of the Divan and shown to the king dead. For it is the custom that he should first see them alive and then dead, and with the blood of his brothers establish the foundations of his kingdom.'

The monument of Suleyman's age is Sinan's great mosque, the Suleymaniye, and one can spend some hours looking at its Alpine beauty descending in domes and turrets and ridges to the dove-coloured stone that lined the streets around with hospitals and schools. In the precinct of the mosque is the tomb of the destructress, Roxelana, too much loved, whose intrigues killed the young heirs and brought her own son to inherit. This sorrow was with the old sultan, and so was the failure of the siege of Malta a year before his end. At seventy-six, he was borne in his litter to the Hungarian wars, and when he died, Sokullu Mehmet Pasha, the Grand Vizier, sent the news in secret to Selim his son. 'For more than seven weeks the great Turkish army of 150,000 soldiers went, and came, and fought, and took towns and cities in the name of the dead man ... and, when the camp was struck, the corpse was placed in the covered litter in which Suleyman had travelled during the campaign, which was now borne along among the troops, surrounded by the customary guards and with all the ceremony and homage which had been shown to the living monarch' (Creasy, p. 196).

This reign touched the height of Osmanli renown and splendour, rich in the civilizations of the great empire that stretched from Atlas to the Caucasus. Its twenty-one governments held most of the famous sites and cities and rivers of the ancient world. Its army had been doubled by Suleyman and was supreme for artillery, and altogether superior in equipment and discipline to anything in the west. Non-Muslims were justly treated and little taxed, and the foreign merchants and their traffic were welcomed; the first Capitulations allowing them their own laws and law-courts were granted to the French in 1535; and while the number of the Janissaries was raised to 20,000, the founding of schools and the exemption of the *ulema* from taxation go to illustrate the care for learning which has appeared in the Levant with every civilization as it rises. The Osmanli state had become the greatest power in both Central Europe and the East.

114, 115–16   The Sultan Han between Aksaray and Konya, built in 1232–36, is one of the best of the 'hans', or inns, by which the Seljuk dynasty marked all the main trade-routes of their vast realms in Asia. At a distance of a day's travel by caravan, one can still trace many of these resting places, all built on the same pattern, with the single gateway opening to a square or rectangle, the arcaded rooms and stable-spaces lining the walls, and the little mosque in the middle.

117, 118, 119   Konya, ancient Iconium, has been the chief centre of the southern plateau from its prehistoric civlization onwards. St Paul visited it three times, and it was the largest town under the Seljuks, before the Mongols came. After their capital had moved from Nicaea to Sivas, they settled in Konya (1134) for some little while between the visits of the First and Second Crusades: a chronicler of the latter describes the city as being about the size of Cologne, with walls and a cathedral. The Crusaders, both in 1097 and in 1190, reached it faint with exhaustion, especially on the second occasion, when they had found neither food nor transport in the grim defiles of the Sultan Dagh; they passed on, after a few days' rest in its unwelcoming gardens, to the coast of Silifke, where their leader, Frederick Barbarossa, was drowned.

When the Seljuk dynasty came to its end, the Karamanlis made Konya their summer capital (after the capture of Alanya, where their winters were spent), and held it until the Ottomans conquered it in 1467.

The Seljuks were great builders everywhere, and particularly so in Konya, and the Karamanlis followed in their footsteps. The great mosque was enlarged and embellished by all the sultans from Alaeddin Keykhubad (1219–36) onwards, and various mosques and schools, and the recognizably Seljuk tombs with their windmill roofs, are still scattered about the town to show what the thirteenth century could do. The little Seljuk mosque known as the Ince Minare Cami ('mosque with the slender minaret') has a richly sculptured doorway (pl. 119) decorated with knotwork, Kufic and foliage motifs. The adjoining school is now a sculpture museum and contains fragments of the old Seljuk city-gate of Konya (pl. 117, 118).

120   The ramparts of Diyarbakir. The great walls with their inscriptions have been pierced here and there by zealous Kaimakams interested in traffic, but the feeling is still one of a fortified gateway to the hills. Many rulers have worked at these walls. The curtains, 26 to 39 feet high and 10 to 16 feet broad, built of masonry rubble between two matching facings, the crenellated parapet and arched gallery under the *chemin de ronde*, the Roman elements still in place between the circular salients of the gates, remain 'the most important and the most complete example of Byzantine fortification of the fourth century' (*Encyclopaedia of Islam*).

The Abbasid period restored the principal gate; the Seljuks, Marwanids and Artukids repaired the western walls and left the great round bastions and inscriptions; and finally the Ottomans concentrated on the citadel.

Inside the town, the Old Mosque (of mixed and controversial origin), Artukid schools, and black and white striped Ottoman mosques (built after the capture of the town in 1514) show among caravanserais and fine-built houses how the prosperity of Amida continued.

121   The Castle of Anamur. This splendidly preserved castle, on a long beach opposite the most southerly headland in Turkey, was built by the Rupenian dynasty of Lesser Armenia in about AD 1230. These Rupenians, after the loss of the Armenian highlands to the Seljuks, descended and reigned for 300 years (1080–1375), scattering their castles along the Cilician coast and up the

slopes of Taurus. The Karamanlis stepped in when the Seljuk power was over, and built their mosque and the two pleasant rooms that still look out to sea from the upper battlements of Anamur. It was called Stamene or Stalimura, and passed from hand to hand in the Crusading ages, until the Ottomans conquered it and left an inscription in 1469.

On the opposite side of the bay are the ruins and tombs of ancient Anemurium; on the south is Cyprus out to sea; and to the north a small pastoral river creeps down from the summer highlands where the villagers take their flocks.

122–3   Konya: the comfortable pattern of the wheat-growing plain. Its productivity is very high and, being now cultivated with the most up-to-date machinery, gives a minimum of two crops a year.

124, 125, 126   The Castle of Hoshap is 35 miles south-east of Van, in lonely country on the Persian border, where the highest vilayet in Turkey leads through the mountains of the Hakkiari to the Tigris. The Hoshap river is here crossed by an old black and white Ottoman bridge, where a precipitous hill holds a fortress containing 380 rooms and cells, two mosques, three baths, prisons, wells, and store-rooms for ammunition and food. This key-point of a frontier was built in 1643.

127, 128, 129   In the vast pastoral stretches of the north-east, and particularly on the slopes and in the valleys east of the Tigris, the Kurds are settled in a semi-nomad manner – in winter villages and, higher up among the pastures, in summer tents. They are among the few people who still wear their traditional costume.

130–1   The typical eastern landscape of Anatolia, its long smooth waves broken and animated by long lines of poplars, or sometimes of willows, beside streams natural or artificial that carry their precious water to the higher cultivation.

132, 133, 134   Van. The new township of Van has been building itself at some little distance from the rock and nearer to the small pier that receives the traffic of the lake. The old city, which was destroyed in the troubles of World War I, has nothing left in its ruin-field except two small Seljuk mosques, with the stone-cut ornament of these northern regions.

Above the plain, the mud-built castle with its more ancient tombs and inscriptions looks out over the lake to two extinct volcanoes on its northern shore. Inside the castle, a mosque, a school, barracks and cisterns are to be found, and 1,000 steps were built by the Seljuks to descend to the plain on the south (the modern, more comfortable, way is on the other side).

135, 136, 137   Edirne (Adrianople) gets its name from the emperor Hadrian, who built it in the second century AD, and it has remained an important centre in the middle of Thrace ever since. After Bursa, when the Osmanlis crossed the Sea of Marmara, it became the second capital of their kingdom, and the plans for the third step, the attack on Constantinople, were studied and made in Edirne. After the removal of the capital to Istanbul, Edirne continued to be of vital importance as an outpost against the Bulgarians; and today it is still flourishing as the most used gateway to Europe.

Markets and mosques and bridges belong to the early days of the Ottoman rule, after the conquest by Murat I in 1361; and it was here that the scarlet background was adopted for the Turkish flag and carried northward for three centuries, from victory to victory across the Balkans, until the tide turned under the walls of Vienna in 1683.

The line of the great sultans fell away miserably after Suleyman the Magnificent, but his generals and especially his Grand Vizier, Sokullu Mehmet Pasha, continued the tradition for a time. Mosques and markets in Edirne are due to the wealth and piety of these early dignitaries, and the prosperous and attractive little town, flourishing with trees and waters in the naked Thracian lanscape, is the chief centre – together with Bursa – for anyone interested in the early architecture of the Osmanlis.

Its most perfect monument, however, belongs to the reign of Selim II: the Selimiye, built by the architect Sinan in 1567–74. One of the most beautiful mosques in the world, it is Sinan's greatest achievement, and floats delicate as a flower over the trees and roofs of Edirne. A wide approach, a painted portico of marble columns, an interior of coloured tiles and windows, and the dome on its eight pilasters are perfect in their harmony; but the greatest beauty is outside, where one can be enchanted by the lightness and serenity of the dome and the grace of the four equal minarets. They climb with three balconies to a height of 260 feet by three inner stairways that never meet until they reach the top.

138, 139   Istanbul. Domes surround the central dome of the Suleymaniye mosque, built by Sinan in 1550–56 under Suleyman the Magnificent. The windows and the coloured inscriptions in this mosque are held to have no equal in their period. Plate 138 shows the small domes round the fountain courtyard, plate 139 one of the subsidiary domes of the mosque.

140, 141, 142   Bursa (Brusa), a little inland from the Marmara southern coast, was the first Osmanli capital. Its citadel had been the ancient stronghold of Prusias, king of Bithynia, who gave it his name and built it (although a legend exists that Hannibal was its founder). In the eleventh century it was an important Byzantine fortress, several times attacked and conquered by the Osmanlis, who besieged it for eleven years and finally took it in 1326. The news of the victory was brought by his son to Othman on his deathbed, and his body was taken to lie on the high citadel under his white turban with his descendants around him. Those not so directly in the line of royalty have their quiet and splendid mausoleums in the lower town, round the house which is still visited as the home of Suleyman the Magnificent.

Up on the hill, with a splendid view over the city, is the Yeshil Cami, or Green Mosque. Built in 1419 by Beyazit's son, Mehmet Çelebi, with his *türbe* (mausoleum) beside it, it takes its name from the colour of the Iznik tiles that decorate the walls of the *türbe*.

143   Istanbul. The mosque of Sokullu Mehmet Pasha, built in 1571 by Sinan, close to the church of SS. Sergius and Bacchus, is one of the most agreeable of the smaller mosques of Istanbul. Tucked into the hill below Sultan Ahmet, its small space is contrived to hold a quiet court of arcaded marble as well as a school, and the interior is pleasantly light, with windows and patterned Iznik tiles grouped here and there like brilliant jewels. Sokullu Mehmet Pasha was the Grand Vizier who held the realm together after Suleyman's death.

144, 145   Bursa. The Ulu Cami, or Great Mosque, in among the bazaars in the lower town below the citadel, was burnt together with the bazaar a few years ago, and has now been restored. It was begun in 1396 and finished in 1400, and is of an old Arab rectangular pattern, with pillars in rows of twelve, holding up twenty cupolas on pointed arches. Under the central cupola, which lets the light in, a fountain splashes into a circular basin.

146   Konya: the Tekke of Mevlana, or Celaleddin al Rumi, the most venerated place of pilgrimage inside Turkey. The monastery of the Mevlevi or Mawlana order of dervishes, which Celaleddin founded, is now a museum; but the tomb close beside it is kept as a holy place, with his turban and the tall, black-felt cylindrical cap of his order upon it. A magnificent cover embroidered with gold and weighing nearly 20 lb is laid over Mevlana and his son.

This poet and mystic was not a native of Konya, but came originally from Balkh on the Oxus. He lived for some years at Laranda (Karaman), where his father had been appointed principal of the university. Reports of the talent of both father and son reached the Seljuk sultan Alaeddin Keykhubad, and in 1231 he invited them to his court in Konya. Celaleddin spent most of the rest of his life in Konya, and it was here too, in 1273, that he died.

117
118

119

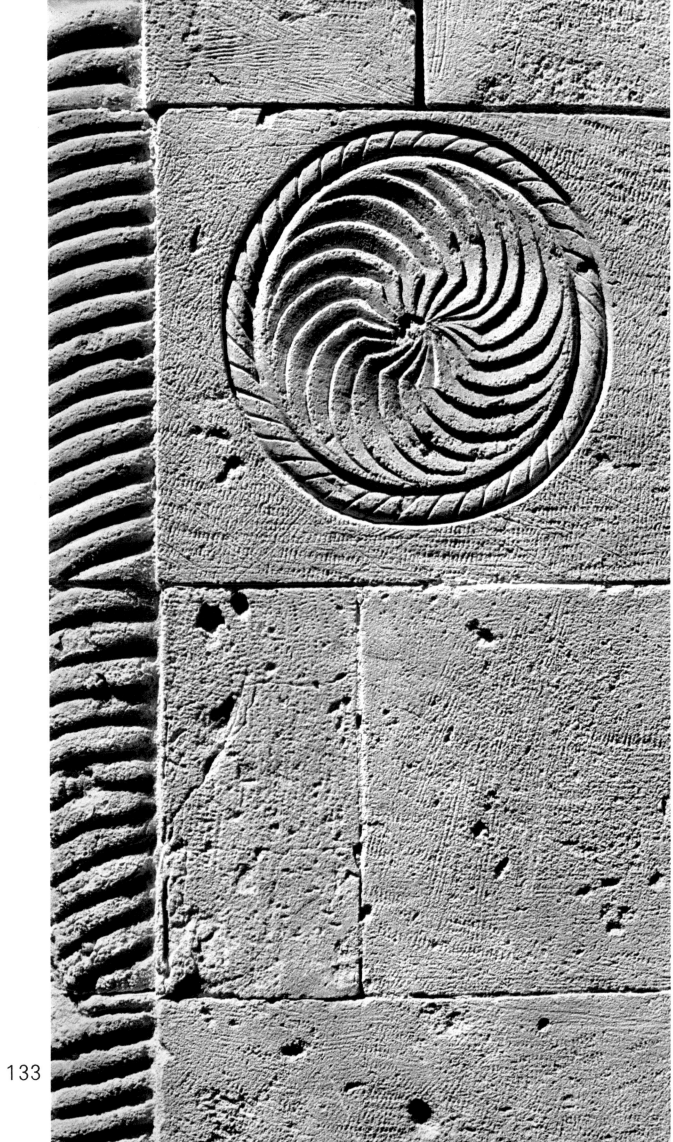

133

141

6 The Ottoman Empire in Decline

When Suleyman died (1566), the half-Russian Selim succeeded; but the work of government and conquest was carried on under the impetus of the dead sultan by his vizier and the veterans of his wars. Cyprus was conquered and peace made with the Venetians; Tunis, like Algiers and Tripoli, came under the Osmanlis; and a new fleet of 250 sail showed that the defeat of Lepanto (1571) had hardly interrupted the Turkish navy in its stride. Yet the limit of expansion had been reached, and two centuries follow of gradual and desperately fought regression. The great sultans were dead; potential successors had been murdered as brothers or nephews, or were carefully secluded, or submerged in the disorders of their time before they could develop. And beyond their new northern frontiers, the Habsburgs in the west and the Russians in the east approach: as early as the fifteenth century, Ivan III had appeared with the last of the Imperial Greek princesses as his wife and the double-headed eagle of Constantinople as his symbol. The slow absorptions of the Turkish conquests become punctuated by treaties ever more disastrous to Islam.

These defeats were not due to any weakening of spirit in the Turkish soldier, who continued to die fighting in battle after battle, and whose revolts were usually inspired by a demand for more warfare rather than less. Nor was there any sign of decadence in populations who resisted desperately, street by street, in their cities (knowing, of course, the horrors that attended the end of a siege). Nor were the viziers who governed nearly as inefficient or corrupt as one would expect from the harem patronage through which they so often came to power. Indeed the second half of the seventeenth century – when Turkey was distracted under the unworthy brother of Murat IV – showed what her democratic bureaucracy could do by producing from the Albanian family of the Kuprülü a series of viziers almost able to control the chaos. The first of them, after twenty-five years as kitchen boy and cook, became Master of the Horse, and later governor in Damascus, Tripoli and Jerusalem. When the mother of the Sultan recommended him to the empire, he was seventy years old and is said to have cleaned the Augean stables by having 36,000 people executed during the five years of his administration. His son ruled Turkey in all but name from 1661 to 1676, and was the greatest of her statesmen; he won the long war for Candia, and put the finances of the empire on their feet, and ended his life with an honourable peace with Poland, keeping the Ukraine. But the armies he led were no longer the best-equipped in the world and he was no general to compete with Montecuculi or Sobieski. Musketeers, pikes and heavy cavalry had been produced by the German wars in the west, and Turkey would have found herself defenceless if Europe had not had sufficient troubles of her own during the seventeenth and eighteenth centuries to prevent her concentrating uninterruptedly on the east.

Turkey's home problems were finance and the Janissaries, who hung over the country throughout these two centuries like Shelley's cloud,

Vaulted with all thy congregated might
Of vapours, from whose solid atmosphere
Black rain, and fire, and hail, will burst

– as it did, at frequent intervals, whenever the Janissaries revolted.

Even under Suleyman they had given trouble, and he had cut down two ringleaders with his own hand; but under his grandson they revolted three times to force the depositions of viziers. In 1622 they murdered the Caliph, whose person had hitherto been held sacred. Sir Thomas Roe, James I's ambassador in Istanbul, describing the country in this same year, writes that 'a man may ride three, four, and sometimes six days, and not find a village able to feed him and his horse; whereby the revenue is so lessened, that there is not wherewithal to pay the soldiers.' He foresees that, when the remedies fail 'which cannot long endure, either the soldiery must want their pay or the number must be reduced; neither of which will they suffer.' (Quoted in Creasy, pp. 200, 245.)

A great and rigid sultan appeared in Murat IV, in 1623. He waited through the terrors of his adolescence and the deaths of his friends till, with long preparation and a Bosphorus strewn with Janissary corpses, he brought the troops to order. What remained faithful he led in the old style to the conquest of Baghdad from the Persians, and came back to ride in triumph through the streets of Istanbul – the last sultan to head his own army. He died at twenty-eight in 1640, and the Janissaries relapsed into their ways.

The financial problem, too, was partly bound up with the army, in so far as the Sipahi cavalry had been a means of economy, their rewards being paid not in cash but in lands ever newly acquired. This could not go on, since the Sipahis were now out of date and could do little against the new weapons and artillery, whose expense was crippling to a nation as sketchily organized as Turkey. Even the geographic dice were now loaded against them: the discovery of the Cape of Good Hope and its seaway had not immediately damaged the old trade-routes of Asia, but was doing so before the end of the sixteenth century: the Mediterranean trade was shrivelling away, and silver pouring from the New World was piling a further Pelion on Ossa upon nations ignorant of economics, whose coinage was rapidly debased.

With all this heaping itself upon her, and Russia ever advancing, the resilience of the people of Turkey was shown in their admirable heroism for decade after decade through two centuries. The second, terribly mismanaged, siege of Vienna (1683) was rightly hailed as a turning-point by a rejoicing Europe, that now converged on Turkey from every available front. The treaties of Carlowitz in 1699, of Passarovitz in 1718, of Kaynarca in 1774 and of Jassy in 1792 mark the stages of retreat, with Russia at last mistress of the Black Sea and Crimea, and the Mediterranean open before her.

Turkey, after Carlowitz and the loss of Belgrade, was no longer feared on her own account; but by that very fact she became an object of general solicitude to the nations of Europe, and offers of mediation were made at intervals by England and Holland and at last accepted. Plenty of powers were not anxious to see the Tsar – and even less so the great Catherine – in Istanbul; and, even to the powers engaged, the defeating of the Turks was extremely costly in lives. The Sultan's armies would be collected, and be thrown away by inadequate generalship as at Vienna and Belgrade (where they had Prince Eugene against them), but the readiness for another war was always there, and the sporadic revolts that became more and more frequent were nearly always inspired by an eagerness for action. The Turkish government too, in the nadir of its fortunes, could stand firm on a point of honour, and refuse the triumphant Tsar's demand that refugees – such as the defeated King of Sweden – should be turned away from their asylum.

Nor were the Turks in their inferiority always beaten. Here and there a treaty took a step backwards and was signed in their favour, and twice in the eighteenth and nineteenth centuries (in the marshes of the Pruth in 1711 and at Adrianople in 1829) they had the Russian army at their mercy and – as if by the opening of a trap – let them escape by treaties ignorantly lenient.

Their virtues as well as their faults worked against them: tenacity and tradition and above all the Gazi faith which had never weakened in its championship of Islam; wholeheartedly exclusive, it was out of touch with the surrounding world. In the teeth of practically every opinion in Europe, in the struggle with every disaster within their borders or beyond them, and with a machine of government that seemed to be dedicated to corruption, the unsubmitting steadfastness of the Turks carried them through. This long history of success and failure has produced the character that is recognized by almost all travellers who get to know the Turk in his own country: 'That dignity of manner, that honourable self-respect, that truthfulness, honesty, and sense of justice, that gentleness and humanity even towards the brute creation, which the bitterest enemies of the Ottomans confess and which is the theme of uniform admiration with foreigners who have been dwellers in the Ottoman empire.' (D'Ohsson, quoted by Creasy, p. 108.)

What the West will do to these virtues, which I have still had the happiness to live amongst, remains to be seen. At the turn of the nineteenth century, Sultan Selim III's small body of western-trained troops, armed with musket and bayonet, drew Napoleon's attention by their firmness at the siege of Acre. Medieval and modern were strangely mingled in this campaign: the (land) battle of Aboukir was lost by the already victorious Turks when they dispersed to collect and cut off their enemies' heads; Napoleon, marching north, had put 2,000 Turkish prisoners to death 'by musketry', in cold blood among the sandhills of Jaffa.

Out of this clash of epochs – stained with the imprisonment and final murder of Selim, and sealed with the long-overdue annihilation (by gunfire) of the Janissaries in their barracks – the new age advanced with steps made cautious by the disapproval of most of the country around it. Selim, in the solitude after his abdication, had been able to hand his western message to his cousin and successor, and Mahmut II waited through eighteen years of chaos and reaction until he was able to bring the tyranny of the Janissaries to an end.

This he did in 1826, and he still had twelve years of rule in which to build the land as he hoped to see it, using the foundations left by Selim: the schools and diplomatic missions, a printing press, and other innovations whose unobtrusive but important influence continued to spread under whatever government there might be. France, Peter the Great, and chiefly Mehmet Ali, verging on rebellion in Cairo, were the signposts for progress, and with a few years of peace his plans might have succeeded. He had an organized army of 40,000 men, trained and fitted out in a western way. But these very facts made Russia aware of the need to hurry, and the bitter treaty of Ackermann was imposed in this same year. Two months later the whole of the Sultan's new navy was wiped out by the European allies at Navarino: 'The Sultan has destroyed his own army and his allies have destroyed his navy', Baron von Moltke reports.

Defenceless as he was, and with anger against the new order seething round him, Sultan Mahmut held on. It was now, in 1829, that the Russians crossed the great Balkan and sent on their ships to wait for them in both the Black and the Aegean Seas. Marshal Diebitsch bluffed his way through plague and dysentery to Adrianople, where another desperate treaty was signed before the Turks discovered that scarcely 13,000 of their enemies were left: another week or so of war, or even of inaction, would have altered the whole face of the situation. In 1830, Algiers was taken by the French, and two years later Muhammad Ali's son was just kept from landing on the Bosphorus by Russians from Odessa. The universal opinion in Europe held Turkey to be dead.

But Sultan Mahmut still had seven years to live, and spent them in the slow and devoted reorganizing of his realm; plans that had long ago been made were continued, and the shattered country was turning, in spite of every internal opposition, slowly to the west. When Mahmut died, in July 1839, the news of his troops' defeat by Mehmet Ali was on its way to him, and he was just spared the sorrow of receiving it: but the powers of Europe, now thoroughly alarmed by the thought of Russia in the Mediterranean, intervened (with the tardiness of which a century and more of experience seems not yet to have cured them). Mehmet Ali kept Egypt, but Syria was handed back to the Sultan, and – more important – the Dardanelles were recognized as Turkish and forbidden to foreign ships of war. The Crimean struggle was in the offing. 'The sick man is dying', Tsar Nicholas said in St Petersburg to Sir Hamilton Seymour; 'we have on our hands a sick man, a very sick man, and he may suddenly die.' 'The hour if not *of* at least *for* his dissolution', was the English ambassador's ironic comment, and Lord Clarendon's dispatch of 23 March 1853 remarks that 'Turkey only requires forbearance on the part of its allies, and a determination not to press their claims in a manner humiliating to the dignity and independence of the Sultan – that friendly support, in short, which among states as well as individuals the weak are entitled to expect from the strong – in order not only to prolong its existence, but to remove all cause of alarm respecting its dissolution.' (Quoted in Creasy, p. 535.)

When the Crimean War was practically ended by the taking of Sebastopol, the Treaty of Paris in 1856 guaranteed the 'territorial integrity of the Ottoman Empire', though the main clause, for the neutralizing of the Black Sea, was repudiated by Russia in 1870, when France became too much involved with Germany to interfere.

Mahmut had two sons and a grandson, Abdul Hamit, who also reigned; and they followed the great sultan's policy in both its branches – eliminating the old to build the new. Now this is the most delicate of all operations, and one in which most reformers fail, and there is a lot to be said for the hand-to-mouth English method, whereby the old is left to trot along beside its innovations, till the pace becomes too quick and it dies of its own accord: when this happens, the new is already installed with a minimum of trouble. But there is nothing the thorough-going reformer dislikes more than to have his route encumbered with relics, and this sweeping away of vestiges is where nearly all his failures begin; and if it has to be done, it should be as Mustafa Kemal was soon to do it, with so strong and rapid a concentration on the *future* that the minds of men would scarcely notice the empty interval that cut them from their past. The best analysis of what happened in Turkey was made by Von Moltke, the keenest and most intimate of the observers, and applies both to Mahmut and his three descendants in their turn:

'It was indispensable for his [Mahmut's] purpose', he says, 'to raze to the ground any other authority within the compass of the Empire and to unite the whole plenitude of power in his own hand; to clear the site before setting up his own building. The first part of his great task the Sultan carried through with perspicacity and resolution; in the second he failed.' (Quoted in Bernard Lewis, *The Emergence of Modern Turkey*, London 1961, p. 124.)

Before every reform, the old was destroyed, its faults and merits bundled out together, and a vast field of anxiety and bitterness was left; and the newly acquired possibilities were added one by one to the Sultan's own power, so that a shadow of absolutism came to darken the landscape of reform and alienate its natural supporters. In 1876, when, after an uncle's abdication and a father's deposition, Abdul Hamit was about to be lifted to the throne, a draft constitution was shown him and approved: but the parliament that met the year after was dissolved in less than a twelvemonth – and thirty years passed before it met again.

Yet much was gained and survived, or was even started during the period of reaction: schools, student missions abroad, the vital reading of newspapers, roads, railways (1856), telegraph (1855), the centralizing of provincial governors' power, the secularizing of education to hedge in the *ulema*, the first university, the abolition of the Sipahis and their *timars* (landed estates), and European clothing for the army (which had led to Selim's deposition eighteen years before); and the Tanzimat, the New Regulations, brought in equality for followers of all religions in the presence of the law – a theory deeply shocking to a nation in which religion, and therefore a basic inequality dependent on choice, had ever been supreme.

All these unpopular shocks brought the movement of reform to a standstill towards the mid-century, while lack of progress and the desperately bankrupt state of the finances perturbed the powers of Europe.

Backwards and forwards half her length
With a short uneasy motion,

the ship of state, like that of the *Ancient Mariner*, was shaken by things that came to it out of long, unmeasured distances of space or time. Meanwhile the Young Turks were eloquent in Paris, and the Bey of Tunis, rather surprisingly, produced the first European constitution among Muslims, and Abdul Hamit had tried it and decided that he preferred to modernize in his own way. He both fostered the policies that derived from his grandfather Mahmut, and developed the westernizing amenities in Turkish life (which were helpful to a centralizing autocracy), while he gagged every effort at reform as soon as it began to blossom; yet the Young Turk movement continued to expand.

By 1906 a small group of officers, with Mustafa Kemal among them, started a revolutionary 'Fatherland and Freedom' society. Such things spread quickly in an army that sees its country racing down to ruin, and mutinies among wretchedly provided soldiers spread quickly too. In 1908 the 'Committee of Union and Progress' came out into the open, based on armies in Macedonia and Edirne; and the Sultan, faced with the threat of a march on the capital and an ultimatum, once more granted a constitution. The wild joy that spread to the farthest corners of the empire is described by Gertrude Bell in *Amurath to Amurath*, as she sets out from Damascus to cross the desert to Baghdad.

Ottoman history, from its first Central Asian irruption, has a keynote of loyalty, to Islam – of which it was the champion – in the first place, and to the family of its rulers in the second: and the new brotherhood of the empire, its faiths and peoples, was up against this most abiding and uncompromising quality of the ruling race. The response to the olive branch offered to the infidel was anyway disheartening: Austria seized Bosnia and Herzegovina, Bulgaria declared herself independent, Crete attached herself to Greece; Italy for 1911, and the Balkan alliance for 1912, were preparing to pounce in their turn; an old-fashioned reaction murdered thousands of Armenians in Cilicia; and the Young Turks, when they got back into the saddle, shed their liberal branches (by both trickery and violence), and entered World War I on the German side under the naked, Turkish-racialist triumvirate of Enver, Talaat and Cemal Pasha. The constitution and its hopes went down in the general welter of ruin. In 1918, with the war lost and the country partitioned, the Committee of Union and Progress was disbanded and its leaders fled; they, too, had brought their panacea to the moment of truth and seen it fail, as all the divergent patriotic efforts of sultans or viziers had failed before them. The deeply divided country, on the verge of annihilation, still tottered at the cross-roads of history: vision and action, irresistible but rarely united, alone could save it; and the Fates were kind, and at this supreme moment inspired the new sultan (Abdul Hamit's younger brother) to send the hero of Gallipoli, the 37-year-old general Mustafa Kemal, as inspector general of the Ninth Army to the Black Sea coast.

The pleasant little town of Giresun – Xenophon mentions it as he marched with his Ten Thousand along the coast – has an old acropolis with walls shaded by plane trees; and a small column, set on the height, records the unnoticed, momentous landing at Samsun in May 1919.

An armistice had been signed at Mudros on HMS *Agamemnon*, and sixty Allied ships were anchored in Istanbul. The French general had ridden into the city on a white horse given him by the Greeks, and a Greek army, landed in Izmir (Smyrna) under cover of the Allied battleships (partly to forestall the Italians), was marching inland. Anatolia, crushed under all the partitions, roused herself at this last stroke to fight with her guerrillas.

Kemal disembarked four days after the Greek landing.

Meetings at Sivas and Erzurum, and the Grand National Assembly in Ankara in April 1920, led to a year of struggle and defeat – fighting against French, Greeks, Armenians, and the government in Istanbul. In 1921 the Turks first drove a Greek force back at İnönü, whence Kemal's friend and successor took his name; in August, Kemal himself defeated the Greeks on the Sakarya river; and, on 9 September 1922, Izmir was retaken. Soviet Russia had made peace; the French and Italians had retreated from their slices of the western coast. Only the English remained on the isthmus which Kemal had to cross if he wished to rescue Thrace. There was a story at the time that he gave orders to his men to march through their lines with arms reversed, confident that no shot would be fired against unarmed men – a pleasant tale if true.

In 1923 the peace of Lausanne was signed; the long inferiority of the Capitulations was abolished, and Turkey left with free sovereignty over practically all that she has today.

The Gazi (as Kemal was known after his victories) spent the rest of his life in consolidating this heritage, resolutely turning from all voices that called from beyond its borders. Conquest is a first step: and the next is a long, exacting round of slow, devoted labour. Here the Tamerlanes of this world, and even the Alexanders have failed; and here Kemal Atatürk (for that was the surname he adopted) showed his most rare greatness.

Perhaps, in his vision, the real size of his undertaking was clear to him from the first? For Turkey was still at the cross-roads, undecided, and he had to turn this great country round, away from all its past, to make it look out of the depth of its distresses into the future, with eagerness and hope. This he did. And he was able to do it because he *was* Turkish – not pan-Islamic, or pan-Turanian, or Balkan, or international Istanbul, but tied by the heart to the inarticulate people whom the centuries had hammered out on their rigid uplands, whose gentleness and loyalty, strength and patience, he could interpret and lead, because it was a part of the material of which he himself was made.

In November 1922 the Sultanate was abolished; in 1923 Ankara became the seat of government, and the Republic was proclaimed. The Caliphate, which had remained, so to say, in the air with the departure of the last sultan, was abolished in 1924, and with it went such venerable institutions as the *sheriat* courts (governed by the Holy Law of Islam) and the Sheyh-ul-Islam (the Chief Mufti in Turkey). Dictatorial powers had to be given for two years after this drastic effort, and were particularly needed when the dervish brotherhoods were banned and the hat was introduced to replace the fez: 'I see a man in the crowd in front of me', said Kemal on the Black Sea coast in 1925; 'he has a fez on his head, a green turban on the fez, a smock on his back, and on top of that a jacket like the one I am wearing. Now what kind of outfit is that?' And the women came off no better, 'who turn their backs and huddle on the ground when a man passes by. ... Gentlemen, can the mothers and daughters of a civilized nation adopt this strange manner, this barbarous posture? It is a spectacle that makes the nation an object of ridicule. It must be remedied at once' (Lewis, pp. 264–5).

One should perhaps in fairness give the other point of view, published by the rector of the Al-Azhar university and the Chief Mufti in Egypt: 'A Muslim, they say, who seeks to resemble a non-Muslim by adopting the latter's distinctive form of dress, will also come to take the same way as he in his beliefs and actions. That is why he who wears the hat because of an inclination to the religion of another and a contempt for his own is an infidel, according to the unanimous opinion of the Muslims' (Lewis, p. 264).

Yet the fez was abolished, and the old-fashioned calendar also, and a new civil code was adopted from the Swiss. By 1928 the Latin script had taken the place of the Arabic, and from 1932 onwards the call to prayer came from the minarets in Turkish, and the loss of the sonorous Arabic words to which people were accustomed seems to have been the greatest shock of all.

Kemal Atatürk died in November 1938, and his stone sarcophagus stands in the mausoleum built for him at Ankara, on a hill beside the town. Ismet Inönü succeeded as president, and kept the country wisely out of war, walking along the tightrope that divided its sympathies between Germany and the Allies. His friendship and that of Kemal had long been for England, and I remember a story told me between the wars by an English officer's wife. She had joined her husband, who was commanding some troops in the conquered Cilician Taurus, which at the end of World War I the French hastened to claim and take over, only to be pushed out by Kemal within a matter of weeks. Her husband told her, that although he had been careful to keep up appearances by sending out his pickets and taking all precautions, he had done so merely as a matter of form, since Kemal had sent a note across the lines to tell him that, while the French would be dislodged if they came, the English would be left alone. Such was the story, and it seemed probable at the time.

In Turkey in general, however, there was, as there always has been, a great deal of sympathy for Germany – who was fighting Russia – and whose murderous racialism was a Tempter's voice to a mixed nation at the cross-roads of her fate. Talaat's Armenian massacres in World War I have been attributed to a casual remark made in Istanbul by General Liman von Sanders; and the 1943 scandal of a capital levy by which the Turkish government denuded her subject races is likely enough to have grown in the same climate of ruthlessness and power; it was not a part of the tradition which belonged to the Osmanli saga.

I first saw Ankara in 1939, a rudimentary capital with few and stunted trees about three feet high. Istanbul had its undying magic, but it could be attained only through precipitous inequalities that led up from Bosphorus or Galata to Pera or Serai, and threatened one's ankles as one walked. A hard poverty was reflected from the empty shops to the quiet people.

I missed the first democratic election in 1950, when the opposition came to power; but I was travelling up the western coast just before the one that followed it in 1954, and saw for myself with what a touching seriousness the simplest village was approaching the responsibility of its vote. In the guest room, among the elders, with the young men on the outer circle as one talked through the evening, the parties (four of them as far as I remember) were discussed, and the families would have decided which one to support, each member for himself. Atatürk had done his work and had based it on the truest Turkish characteristic, the need to serve with every strength, through every sacrifice, the creed that it believes in. It had been Islam and the Osmanli house through seven centuries or more; it is now the nation and government of their land. Before he died, they told me, the Gazi had charged the young men to see to it that there must never again be a dictator in Turkey – and the Menderes crisis and its drastic resolution must be looked at in this light.

Coming to the end of my short synthesis of one of the noblest of the world's histories, I hope my readers will join me in wishing this honourable and beautiful country a long and happy future worthy of its past.

147 Ankara (Ancyra) is not only the capital but also the symbol of modern Turkey. A few decades ago it was a small provincial town; the trees planted in what were to become its future avenues were scarcely four foot high, and it contained neither a good hotel nor restaurant. Now it is a modern metropolis, with boulevards, parks, public and private buildings, university, parliament, opera and museum. It is dominated by two hills. On one of them is the old citadel, which goes back to prehistoric times and incorporates features from every period, from Roman to Ottoman. On the other is the new Atatürk Monument, seen here, only completed after World War II. Atatürk's tomb is in the sombre porticoed building in the centre. In front of it is a large paved space used for public ceremonies, and to the left an impressive avenue leading to the city.

Mustafa Kemal Atatürk was based on Ankara from 1919 onwards, when the Congress of Sivas, which he organized, moved the seat of the revolutionary government. In October 1923, he obtained the proclamation of the Republic and was elected its first President.

148, 149 Smyrna (Izmir). The city is spread along a bay dominated by a magnificent chain of mountains. The Etruscans are said by Herodotus to have sailed from this shore to reach the Tyrrhenian Sea, and when the years had passed, Alexander came and is said to have fallen asleep under a tree and to have been advised by Nemesis in his dream to build the city on the higher ground where the ancient walls still stand. The old city stretches down from this height, with marble slabs of columns still scattered here and there among its steep streets and small houses, and an agora, and above it the shapeless hollow which was once the stadium where St Polycarp was burned (he was brought here late in the day, when the games were over and no hungry lions were left).

The siege of Tamerlane, the division of the town between Muslim and Crusader, all left their mark – but the most enduring was probably the fire of 1922, when Mustafa Kemal Atatürk descended on the burning city and the Greek army was chased into the sea. This was the seal of his victory, and the new prosperity is only now covering the traces of all these 'old, unhappy, far-off things' which Smyrna begins to forget as she celebrates her Annual Fair and adds treasures to her well-kept museum.

150, 151 Kirkpinar, near Edirne, is one of the centres for wrestling matches. The Turks have no categories for weight, and most of their wrestlers are either heavyweight or medium. A bout between them sometimes lasts for a very long time; all holds and all punches are permitted so long as the adversary is forced to the ground. The oiled bodies slip away under the hand, and one might imagine the attacks to be only preambles to the real struggle, meant to relax the muscles and rub away any excessive oil while waiting for some sign of fatigue or inattention in the adversary. One is free to catch hold of anything, even the edge of the wrestler's garment, wherever a hold can be contrived. The faces are covered with sweat and oil, and at every round the trainer rushes to wash them so that the combat may continue. The victor is the one who can force his opponent's shoulders to touch the ground with his face turned upwards.

When this has happened, the victor has to step in again almost at once, and it is only after three consecutive victories, as in ancient Greece, that he can enjoy his honours. It looks as if this Turkish tradition of wrestling goes back to the forms and influences of ancient Greece.

152 Anatolia is climatically divided into four distinct

zones: three are coastal – the Levant, the Aegean and the Pontic – and one is the interior, a plateau shut away from all the friendly activities of the sea. The southern is the hottest among the coastal zones, and its most profitable cultivation is that of cotton, most particularly grown in the plain of Adana. The Aegean slopes grow the typically warm-temperate products, such as vines, greens, figs (to be dried) and pistachio nuts. Raisins and currants, the pipless *sultanina* grape, are important, and in 1968 were producing about six million cwt per annum.

153 Everywhere in Turkey, but especially on the Anatolian plateau, the cultivation of wheat is widespread. The annual production is about a hundred million tons.

154, 155, 156 Bursa: the Yenikaplica. These baths were built by the sixteenth-century Grand Vizier Rustem Pasha during the reign of Suleyman the Magnificent, on the site and with many of the materials of their Byzantine predecessors. The central room is an octagon, opening onto eight rooms whose walls are covered with very original turquoise tiles. In the middle is a marble basin, where the water pours in between the four Byzantine columns that support the dome of the ceiling. The towels, woven in Bursa (still famous for its weaving), are hung out of doors to dry.

157 The semi-nomad women and their children on the montain pastures east of Lake Van. They lead the healthiest life through the easy summer days among the flowers, and come back to winter in their villages only when the grazing for their flocks gives out. This photograph shows a typical scene in the countryside. Groups of women, accompanied by their smaller children, leave the village in order to meet and talk on one of the hillocks nearby.

158 The camel caravan, with the donkey leading it, is still frequent along the Aegean and southern coasts, and there are, in fact, plenty of steep tracks leading into the Taurus valleys where it is still the safest, and perhaps eventually the quickest, mode of transport. These are unloaded camels with the wooden saddle, alongside whose pommels the voluminous bales are slung.

159 Mardin, high on its hill, dominates the Mesopotamian plain. Under its ancient name of Marida or Maridus, it stood on the frontier of the Hittite empire. It came later under the Mitanni (ancestors of the Kurds) in the north, then under Babylon and Asshur in the south, and finally under Persia, Alexander the Great,

and Rome. Conquered by the Arabs in AD 640, it was taken and made their capital city by the Artukoglu in 1096; until finally the Ottomans annexed it.

All this history produced a great deal of good building, for which Mardin has continued to be well known in modern times; indeed it is only the whiteness of the stone that can always distinguish the old from the new. It has a *türbe* (mausoleum) or two, and some fine strips of Byzantine carving; but its finest monument is the fourteenth-century school, the Sultan Isa Medrese, with its great portal and double-domed buildings under the citadel on the flat-topped hill.

160, 161 The forest-clad coast of the Black Sea is very different from any other region in Turkey, and its products are different also. Tobacco is widely grown, especially around Samsun, and is much valued, its production having reached about four million cwt in 1968.

162–3 A few cows, goats and hens make up the wealth of these villagers. In backward areas it is quite customary for the women to turn their faces away from photographers, as they are doing here.

164 Opium poppies are grown in the region of Amasya, and particularly in that of Afyon Kara Hisar, a striking place with a high rock and a castle full of ancient fragments. It is also famous as the place where Alcibiades was attacked in the night while he slept, and was killed.

165 Maize, recently introduced to the Black Sea region from Rize, is flourishing.

166–7 The wide volcanic valleys of the plateau of east Turkey around Erzurum. On these smooth, high mountains there is little vegetation above 5,000 feet, and there is a sharp break between the cultivated, communal wheatfields and the brown rock melting into a purple distance. The atmosphere, too, seems thinner and paler, and this strange, simple and majestic landscape characterizes the whole of these austere regions of the northeast of Turkey.

168 The tourist village built by the Club Européen du Tourisme in the bay of Kushadasi. In the last few years Turkey has rapidly been becoming a holiday ground, a landscape for mass tourism. When one mentions Turkey, one no longer thinks only of Istanbul; charter flights now procure a fortnight's bathing from a modern hotel in Alanya, or on the bay of Kushadasi. Yet, for all this, one may say that Turkey keeps her true secrets, and is a land still to be discovered.

159

168

Principal Dates and Index

Principal Dates

527–565	Reign of Justinian I
548	Church of St Sophia completed
663, 673–8, 717	The Arabs besiege Constantinople
867–1056	Byzantine expansion in the north-east
1071	Battle of Manzikert. Earliest penetration of Seljuk Turks into Asia Minor
1078–1097	First Seljuk Emirate of Anatolia established at Nicaea
1081–1204	Comnenus dynasty
1096–1097	The First Crusade comes to Constantinople and crosses Asia Minor
1097–1300	The Seljuk Sultanate, at Konya
1204	Constantinople sacked by the Crusaders (Fourth Crusade)
1204–1261	Greek government at Nicaea and Frankish government at Constantinople
1261	Constantinople recaptured by the Byzantines
1261–1453	Palaeologus dynasty
1326	Bursa becomes the first Ottoman capital
1357	The Ottoman Turks cross into Europe
1367	Adrianople becomes the new Ottoman capital
1402	Tamerlane defeats the Ottoman sultan Beyazit at the Battle of Ankara
1453	Siege and capture of Constantinople by Mehmet II (5 April–29 May)
1520–1566	Suleyman the Magnificent. The Ottoman Empire reaches the height of its power and splendour
1550–1556	Construction of the Suleymaniye complex
1597–1618	Ahmet I. The Sultan Ahmet mosque
1703–1730	Ahmet III. The 'Tulip Period'
1789–1807	Selim III. First attempts at reform
1826	Massacre of the Janissaries
1829	The Russians enter Adrianople
1839	The Gul-Hane Charter, initiating a period of reforms (Tanzimat)
1841	The Straits Convention
1856	Treaty of Paris. New charter of reforms
1868	Franco-Turkish Lycée opened at Galata-Saray
1876–1909	Abdul Hamit II, the 'Red Sultan'
1908	Revolution of the Young Turks
Oct. 1918	Armistice of Mudros; Ottoman Empire dismembered
1919–1922	Mustafa Kemal and the War of Independence
July 1923	Treaty of Lausanne
Oct. 1923	Proclamation of the Republic of Turkey, with Mustafa Kemal as President
1924	The Caliphate abolished
Nov. 1938	Death of Mustafa Kemal Atatürk
1938–1950	Ismet Inönü, second President of the Republic
May 1950	Democratic government, with Djelal Bayar as President
May 1960	Military coup, followed by free elections in 1961

Index